Studying Students:
The Undergraduate Research Project at the University of Rochester

Edited by

Nancy Fried Foster

Susan Gibbons

Association of College and Research Libraries
A division of the American Library Association
Chicago 2007

The paper used in this publication meets the minimum requirements of American National Standard for Information Sciences–Permanence of Paper for Printed Library Materials, ANSI Z39.48-1992. ∞

Library of Congress Cataloging-in-Publication Data

Studying students : the Undergraduate Research Project at the University of Rochester / edited by Nancy Fried Foster and Susan Gibbons.
    p. cm.
 Includes bibliographical references and index.
 ISBN 978-0-8389-8437-6 (pbk. : alk. paper)
 1. University of Rochester. River Campus Libraries--Case studies. 2. University of Rochester--Students--Case studies. 3. Academic libraries--Use studies. 4. Report writing. 5. Research. 6. Study skills. I. Foster, Nancy Fried. II. Gibbons, Susan (Susan L.), 1970-

 Z733.U868S78 2007
 025.5'877--dc22

                  2007028559

Printed in the United States of America.

11 10 09 08 07   5 4 3 2 1

Contents

Introduction to the Undergraduate Research Project

Nancy Fried Foster and Susan Gibbons

The University of Rochester's River Campus Libraries are known as innovative and forward thinking, especially in the areas of reference outreach, online catalogs, institutional repositories, and Web-based services. Still, the library staff wanted to do more to reach students and their instructors in support of the university's educational mission. But to do more, we realized we needed to know more about today's undergraduate students—their habits, the academic work they are required to do, and their library-related needs. In particular, we were interested in how students write their research papers and what services, resources, and facilities would be most useful to them. As Katie Clark, director of the Carlson Science and Engineering Library, remarked early in this project, "Papers happen," but we did not know how they happen.

Thus, in the summer of 2004, a group of librarians and the River Campus Libraries' lead anthropologist met at a park on the shore of Lake Ontario for lunch and a discussion of some research we might do to enlarge our knowledge of undergraduate work processes. Many of us had participated in a previous study, supported by a grant from the Institute for Museum and Library Services, to examine the work practices of faculty members in order to build a better institutional repository (Foster and Gibbons 2005). Based on the success of that study, we decided to use similar anthropological and ethnographic methods to examine how undergraduate students write their research papers. The information collected in this study would guide the libraries' efforts to improve library facilities, reference outreach, and the libraries' Web presence.

Defining the Problem

Our first task was to identify one trenchant research question to guide the project. The question we developed was, What do students *really* do when they write their research papers? Between the assignment of a research paper and the finished, submitted product was a black box that largely concealed the processes undertaken by the student. We wanted to take a peek into that box to see what we could find. We felt that this question accurately reflected our ignorance of student work habits while providing a manageable focus for our information-gathering activities.

We took a general approach, avoiding presuppositions. We wanted to begin our project by exploring students' practices; we did not set out to prove a point. Our initial aim was to be able to describe in detail how students actually write their research papers. This would enable the library staff to develop new ways to help students meet faculty expectations for research papers and become adept researchers.

Nancy Fried Foster is Lead Anthropologist at the River Campus Libraries at the University of Rochester; e-mail: nfoster@library.rochester.edu. Susan Gibbons is Associate Dean, Public Services and Collection Development at the River Campus Libraries at the University of Rochester; e-mail: sgibbons@library.rochester.edu

Laying the Groundwork

Once we had decided to conduct the research, we submitted complete documentation of project goals, methodologies, and protocols to the University of Rochester's Research Subjects Review Board and received the board's approval for the study. Participation in the study was completely voluntary. Each student signed a consent form prior to participating and understood that s/he could withdraw at any time without explanation. Students also gave us permission to reproduce photographs, maps, and drawings in this book.

Approach

Before we actually talked to any students, we wanted to understand what their instructors expected of them, so we created a set of questions to ask faculty members. These questions concerned:

- Hallmarks of a good research paper
- How instructors expect students to find books and articles for their research papers and assignments
- How librarians can help students complete their research papers and assignments
- Obstacles to successful completion of research papers and assignments

In Chapter 1, Barbara Alvarez and Nora Dimmock review the methods, findings, and applications of this study of faculty expectations.

Once we were able to add an understanding of student practices with these faculty expectations, we anticipated that we would want to implement changes or improvements in three major areas: reference outreach, facilities, and Web services. Accordingly, we created three subteams to investigate the questions that seemed to us most important.

For example, in the area of reference outreach, we sought to learn:

- What steps students take when they work through their assignments and write their papers
- Successful and unsuccessful research and planning strategies
- Library and nonlibrary resources that students commonly use
- The differences between the successful strategies of high-achieving students and the experiences of overwhelmed students
- Where students go for help

In Chapter 2, Vicki Burns and Kenn Harper describe interviews conducted at the reference desk and, later, in the student union, to understand how and why students approach the reference desk, when they avoid it, and where else they go to get help. Suzanne Bell and Alan Unsworth delve into the data in Chapter 3 to describe one particular pilot program in which librarians adjusted their hours to accommodate students by staying on the reference desk until 11 P.M. during student crunch times.

A second subteam examined how students use the libraries' facilities and other campus locations, and what effects space and furnishings have on student research and writing practices. We wanted to look at these issues:

- When and why students choose the library as a physical space, and when and why they work elsewhere
- Which parts of the library students like best or least, and why
- What students wish the library had, allowed, facilitated, or provided

In Chapter 4, Susan Gibbons and Nancy Fried Foster discuss the methods we used to collect this information, some of our insights, and the ways we are applying our new knowledge and skills in a major library renovation project.

The third subteam explored how students use our website and other websites, and how that information might help us improve our Web presence. We started out asking

- What students need to do on the Web
- How the library fits into their Web usage
- What students do online and what more they *wish* they could do online
- How the library website does or does not meet student needs for doing their research papers and assignments

Jane McCleneghan Smith and Katie Clark review the methods and results of the two student design workshops we held to answer these questions in Chapter 5.

Additional Investigations

There was so much we wanted to know that we added research activities. One of our greatest challenges was to learn more about the students' academic activities outside of the library and the nine-to-five workday. We had great success asking students to document these times and places for us and then engaging them in discussions about the resulting photos, maps, and drawings. We also conducted interviews late at night, in student dorms, to learn more about how students use their computers and to capture the sights and sounds of residential life.

In Chapter 6, Judi Briden reviews a method we developed for using student photographs as a means of learning more about those parts of their lives that are otherwise inaccessible to us. Katie Clark describes yet another approach we took to gain insight on the students' days in Chapter 7. Using campus maps, students traced out their movements for us during an entire day. In this chapter we see the method and some of our surprising findings.

What It All Means

The final four chapters of this book take a few steps back to discuss some of the project's higher-level findings. Some of these findings relate to our own staff and the effects of participation on their attitudes and understandings. In Chapter 8, Helen Anderson and Ann Marshall discuss the inclusive nature of the project and how this led to new and better working relationships among library staff and to improved relations between library staff and students.

Today's undergraduate students are very different from past generations of college students. In Chapter 9, Sarada W. George pulls out some of the interesting characteristics of the undergraduates who participated in our study. She also reviews the literature on past and current generations of college students and discusses how our local findings accord with the conclusions of other studies.

In Chapter 10, Nancy Fried Foster draws on information gathered throughout the project to examine how service means different things to librarians and students and to draw out the implications of those differences for libraries.

Our concluding chapter suggests how local user studies, such as our Undergraduate Research Project, are a necessary component of any student-centered academic library.

Acknowledgements

The authors of these chapters write on behalf of a much larger group of people who attended meetings, held video camcorders, checked transcripts, brainstormed ideas, and participated in many other ways in this project. We acknowledge with gratitude the work of Jody Asbury, Margaret Becket, Charlie Bush, Sue Cardinal, Diane Cass, Ellen Cronk, Michael DiMauro, Chris Finger, Stephanie Frontz, Denise Hoagland, Mary Huth, Isabel Kaplan, David Lindahl, Diana Luce, Kathy McGowan, Lorraine Porcello, Shirley Ricker, Deborah Rossen-Knill, Nancy Speck, and Dan Watts. We thank Dean Ronald Dow and Associate Dean Stanley Wilder for material and moral support. And we thank more than one hundred students who graciously allowed us into their dorms, took photographs, made maps, drew pictures, and participated in interviews so that we could understand how they write their papers.

one. Faculty Expectations of Student Research

Barbara Alvarez and Nora Dimmock

Before we embarked on our study of how undergraduates at the University of Rochester research and write their papers, we needed a better sense of what students are asked to do when they are assigned research projects. Moreover, we needed more knowledge of the expectations of the faculty and instructors who evaluate the results of their work. Is there any consistency of those expectations across the institution or across disciplines? What kind of research materials are students expected to find and work with? What is a good research paper, anyway? We hoped that by answering these questions we would not only gain insight into what students are expected to accomplish but also discern the most effective ways librarians can help students meet faculty expectations for research papers and become adept researchers.

Findings of Previous Studies

Several studies have looked at faculty expectations of students' research using a variety of methodologies. Valentine (2001) interviewed both undergraduate students and their professors to identify connections, if there were any, between faculty expectations and student commitment. She found that faculty members assign research papers for a variety of reasons, including providing students with the experience of writing in the discipline and giving them a chance to be creative. They grade those papers on the basis of subjective, intangible factors including "legitimate effort" (110). This led Valentine to conclude that faculty members have varied, and sometimes vague, expectations of student work, but that students strive to discern those expectations in order to get good grades.

A study at Bucknell University (Carlson 2006) showed that faculty expectations vary according to the academic discipline and, in general, are lower for introductory courses. Carlson looked at the citation behavior of students by class year and academic disciplines and concluded that instructors' expectations increase as students progress through the curriculum of their major. The academic discipline of the course students were enrolled in also proved an important factor. Students in humanities courses focused heavily on books. Students in social science courses cited more journal articles and websites and overall included more sources than students in the humanities and in foundation seminars.

Another study of the citation behavior of undergraduate students (Davis 2003) revealed the positive effect of faculty guidelines for research on the types and overall number of sources used. Davis looked at the bibliographies of students in an elementary economics class and discovered that the number of book citations dropped from 30 percent in 1996 to 16 percent in 2001, which he attributed to

Barbara Alvarez is Modern Languages and Cultures Librarian at River Campus Libraries, University of Rochester; e-mail: balvarez@library.rochester.edu. Nora Dimmock is Head, Multimedia Center at River Campus Libraries, University of Rochester; e-mail: ndimmock@library.rochester.edu.

1

increased use of the Internet. However, when the professor provided guidelines on appropriate research sources, the number of Web resources dropped dramatically. Davis's study demonstrates how clearly stated faculty expectations can have a direct impact on students' attempts to find and use relevant scholarly literature.

The effect of library instruction on student research skills was the focus of a 2002/3 survey (Singh 2005). Singh surveyed more than four hundred faculty members teaching undergraduates. Although 55.2 percent of faculty believed that library instruction improved students' research processes and 33.8 percent "found their students' research skills to be poor," only 8.6 percent made library instruction a part of their coursework. Singh concluded that many faculty members expect students to have better library skills but few provide the necessary library instruction.

Methodology of Our Study

With the information from some of these past studies in hand, we sought a means to explore the expectations of the University of Rochester faculty for their students' research and writing abilities. To obtain the most exhaustive and, at the same time, most spontaneous answers to our questions, we opted for face-to-face interviews with faculty. A group of subject librarians volunteered to identify professors who had assigned research projects during the current semester and to approach them with interview requests. Fourteen faculty members from a wide range of academic disciplines (six in humanities, five in social sciences, and three in science/technology) agreed to participate in our study.

All of the librarians who volunteered to conduct faculty interviews attended a short training session in ethnographic interview techniques with the libraries' lead anthropologist. An interview protocol provided us with the main points

Table 1.1. Summary of Faculty Interview Responses
Hallmarks of a good paper
• meets goals of the assignment
• good topic: doable and interesting
• well thought out: clear thesis statement, well-developed arguments in relation to the sources used
• well written: no mechanical errors (grammar, spelling); appropriate style for the discipline; appropriate style and content for the intended audience
• well organized and presented: beginning, middle, end; right things in the right section of the paper
• appropriate, high-quality sources
• no plagiarism
• shows understanding of the subject, critical thought, interest, and creativity
How students are supposed to find resources
• independently
• work with other students
• follow instructor's suggestions on how and where to find sources (on syllabi, handouts, writing guides, and at individual meetings)
• use skills learned in a bibliographic instruction session
• ask a librarian for help
• use library's tools and services: databases, catalogs, interlibrary loan
• follow references cited in the textbook and other readings
• get resources from instructor's own collection of books and articles
• use Internet (as long as the quality of visited sites is acceptable)

Table 1.1. Summary of Faculty Interview Responses
What librarians can do to help students
• show how to search subject-specific and interdisciplinary databases
• create guides to subject literature
• explain different research methodologies
• restructure bibliographic instruction: offer more frequent and shorter sessions, more focused on a particular type of resource
• offer library tours at the beginning of the school year
• work closely with faculty
• help with identifying print sources and finding them in stacks
• help with interlibrary loan requests
• encourage persistence, nurture excitement for the topic
• offer reserves and required readings in multiple copies
• help with writing problems
Obstacles to good research papers
• poor time management skills
• problems with formulating arguments and developing a topic
• lack of critical judgment and of reflection upon the sources
• poor understanding of the material
• poor writing skills: declining grammar, inappropriate style for the discipline, no previous experience in scholarly writing, lack of clarity
• plagiarism, often unintentional
• poor choice of topic and lack of focus
• giving up easily
• not enough or poor-quality sources
• pursuing only sources in our collection or online (not using interlibrary loan)
• no experience in working with primary sources
• intimidation by resources
• not knowing how to work with references or cite sources

for discussion but also left room for any additional questions and comments the conversation would afford. Most of the subject librarians took advantage of this excellent opportunity and learned a great deal about student-faculty interaction—much more than we had anticipated at this early point in our project.

The timing of the interviews was crucial. Aiming for the end of the semester, when papers would be due, ensured that most of the faculty were engaged in the process of grading the research assignments and therefore could provide us the most authentic and detailed information. But this timing also created a difficulty because our demand for their time was an added burden. We approached faculty with a strict time limit of forty-five minutes and reassured them at the beginning of the interview that we were cognizant of their time constraints and would be diligent in keeping to our agreed-upon time limit.

Interview Protocol

Our interview protocol had us focus on faculty members who expected to receive research papers from students within a few weeks. We asked them about the hallmarks of a good research paper in general, and what they would look for in this term's papers. We also asked how these faculty members expected students to find books and articles as they worked on the assigned papers, and whether they expected students to get help, and from whom. Finally, we solicited ideas on the ways librarians at the reference desk might be most helpful at this point in the semester, when students were writing their research papers.

Findings

The results of faculty interviews were collected and disseminated to the project team. After looking at the tabulated results we immediately realized that, although there were common threads across all the interviews, our study revealed no evidence of any significant consistency of faculty expectations, either across the institution or at a discipline level. There were also as many distinct answers to each of the questions as there were interviews, and some were even contradictory (see Table 1.1). Such lack of consistency—confirmed later in interviews with students—often puts undergraduates at a loss when they are trying to understand what scholarly investigation and writing are all about. Professors agree that high school training is far from sufficient in preparing students for research pursuits at the college level. For example, two of the interviewed professors told us that they do not expect undergraduates to know how to find books and articles, and that they tend to provide all the materials necessary for the students' projects.

By and large, professors expect students to understand the purpose of the assignment, choose an appropriate topic, and write a cogent and well-supported paper. Frequently mentioned hallmarks of a good paper include an interesting topic, high-quality sources and their proper attribution, demonstrated understanding of the subject and critical thought, well-developed thesis and argumentation, good organization and presentation, and impeccable writing.

The faculty members share the general opinion that graduate students know how to do research, but they are unable to articulate to us how the students attain these skills as undergraduates. Some instructors assume that librarians are teaching research methods at some point, even if the instructors themselves do not request such instruction for their classes. Some assume that a required writing course or a single library session (or both) is sufficient as a basis for the student's entire college career. Consequently, most of the interviewed instructors expect their undergraduate students to know how to find research materials without ever teaching these skills or having any clear idea of how students are supposed to learn them.

In many cases, however, faculty expectations go beyond the mere basics of research and writing. One faculty member explained, "Actually, I expect the students to do something similar to what I do, which is a combination of library resources, … and what can be found on the Internet, and work with references." Not surprisingly, professors implicitly wish that students imitated their own research and writing styles. Yet their ways of conducting research are highly individual and often rely heavily on sources unavailable to students (e.g., peer groups) rather than on traditional library-based tools (Washington-Hoagland and Clougherty 2002, 127). Although they are experts in their own fields, faculty members are not necessarily expert searchers or heavy users of library catalogs and databases, and therefore they may not be prepared to train students in information-finding skills (Barry 1997). At the same time, many are also reluctant to give up scarce class time for bibliographic instruction offered by a librarian.

Even though the faculty members all agreed that locating appropriate scholarly sources is important, their opinions are divided as to the students' skills at finding good resources. Some professors believe that students are quite resourceful and able to find things independently. Others assume that students are already familiar with the databases and Web resources in the subject area. Some do not expect students to do independent research; instead, these instructors provide students with all the materials they need or direct them to selected subject bibliographies. In the minority of classes where bibliographic instruction is taught by a librarian, the instructors believe the session in the library gives the students sufficient training in the use of subject-specific databases and prepares them to become proficient searchers.

When discussing their expectations, faculty commented more extensively on the problems of writing and critical thinking than on those related to locating the right sources. Evaluating and interpreting the information appear much more difficult for students than finding it. Without exception, all interviewed faculty agree that one of the main failures of the research papers they grade is lack of critical judgment. To start with, many students cannot discern the quality of the sources they find and, in consequence, make a poor selection. They lack the sophisticated analytical and interpretive skills they would need to see implicit and explicit relations between the sources or to distinguish between strong and weak arguments.

Second, students tend to summarize readings instead of reflecting upon them and writing critical, thoughtful papers. As one of the professors remarked, it is difficult "to get them to realize they're not there to just repeat what someone else has said, but to internalize and spit back out in their own words, to provide their own 'take' on it … a personal reaction, not just paraphrasing." Trained in high school to write reports, undergraduates do not know how to formulate good research questions and work with the sources in a manner that will produce interesting and coherent answers. While working with the research materials, many students

do not understand the imperative of proper citations and may plagiarize, even if it is completely unintentional.

Finally, all interviewed faculty complained about mechanical problems that plague students' writing: "florid, overwrought language, jumbled and verbose"; "grammar declining over the years"; spelling mistakes; lack of clarity; poor organization of the text; inappropriate style for the discipline or intended audience. In the faculty's opinion, bad writing is an acute problem that turns out to be the main obstacle to students' success in research.

Conclusions

The small number of interviews prevented us from making too many demands on the collected data, but our study led us to several interesting findings and pointed out areas for further exploration. The benefits from the interviews went beyond providing the groundwork for the Undergraduate Research Project by mapping the expectations faculty members have of their students. Most librarians used the interviews as an extension of their liaison activities and interviewed faculty members in their areas of subject expertise. The meetings with faculty offered librarians an excellent opportunity for developing existing relationships or for engaging with faculty they had not had a chance to work with earlier. The librarians learned a great deal more about the classes and assignments they had heard about at the reference desk. Prior to the interviews, two of the instructors did not understand what librarians could do for a class and for individual students. The interview with the subject librarian opened up a new avenue for collaboration and, in several cases, the interviews were followed by the faculty member requesting greater participation by the librarian in a course.

The faculty interviews also provided an opportunity for subject or reference librarians to look more holistically at the process students go through to complete an assignment and to gain a better understanding of their common challenges. In this process, research and writing are deeply intertwined and cannot be separated from each other. Good researchers have to be good writers to present the fruits of their investigation to the scholarly community effectively. Therefore, the help we can offer students has to take into consideration all the elements of success: finding information, understanding and analyzing it, and presenting it in writing.

Librarians can help students in all the steps along the way, starting with bridging the gap of understanding by helping the student figure out "what the professor wants." This requires us to be proactive in communication with faculty about their assignments and the educational goals of the course. It may also necessitate that we augment our methods of bibliographic instruction, offering it not only in more traditional "library sessions" but also in a variety of other fashions. For example, the interviews encouraged us to experiment with special office hours and reinforced the value of the library resource guides that we tailor for individual classes each semester.[1]

Last but not least, the faculty interviews made clear the need for librarians to understand the pedagogy of writing in order to assist students through the final steps of preparing a well-crafted research paper. This conclusion has been reinforced by a collaboration with the University of Rochester College Writing Center.[2] The involvement of our librarians in the College Writing Center programs has been growing in recent years in such areas as research instruction for freshmen and upper-level writing courses, the training of new writing instructors, and the sharing of research and expertise.

As a result of this initial success, eight subject librarians undertook formal training as writing consultants; four now hold regular weekly tutoring hours in the writing center. The writing initiative led to the creation of a specialized tutoring service in Spanish, built upon the language skills and abilities of the modern languages and cultures librarian. Further efforts to connect research and writing led to hiring an undergraduate writing fellow to provide assistance at the reference desk and in bibliographic instruction sessions. In the fall 2007 semester, the libraries' political science librarian will teach her first class as an official freshmen writing seminar instructor. These experiences have also inspired several of us to conduct research on library/writing program collaborations (e.g., Alvarez 2007; Marshall 2006; Ricker and Kaplan 2006).

Our writing center collaboration has been extremely positive, and the feedback suggests that the expansion of our expertise into writing is important, useful, and quite in line with our educational mission. As one librarian puts it, "The excursion into [writing] allows us to reevaluate our professional practice from a broader perspective so that we can support our students and faculty in the most meaningful way" (Alvarez 2006).

The faculty interviews, along with the many other activities associated with the Undergraduate Research Project, have provided us with an opportunity to look at our professional practice from a broader perspective and through the eyes of the students. This, in turn, has allowed us to align our programs and services with student needs and work practices and to provide truly student-centered support for learning.

Notes

1. https://www.library.rochester.edu/index.cfm?page=courses.
2. http://writing.rochester.edu/help/wconsultants.html.

two. Asking Students about Their Research

Vicki Burns and Kenn Harper

The staff of the River Campus Libraries believe that students' literature research can be significantly aided by consultation with information experts, in particular librarians. The Undergraduate Research Project provided us with a way to test that belief and improve the ways we make contact with students. Early in the project, we formed a reference subteam to evaluate students' experience seeking assistance from the reference desk. The subteam consisted of one library assistant and four librarians, representing the sciences and humanities; the project's anthropologist was an ex-officio member of the subteam.

Reference Desk Survey

The subteam began by designing a survey for undergraduates who came to the reference desk at either the main humanities and social sciences library or the science and engineering library to seek help with a research paper. The subteam designed the survey instrument (Appendix 2.1), drew up detailed procedures, and pretested the survey with two student employees to ensure that the questions were clear. The survey was designed to gather basic information about the student and the assignment that brought him/her to the reference desk, as well as the student's motivation to come to the desk and expected outcomes. Students were invited to complete the survey at the end of their encounter at the reference desk, and as a "thank-you" they received a small

flashlight in the shape of a carabiner with "River Campus Libraries" printed on it. To enhance the survey we sent each student two follow-up e-mails, one within a few days and one after the completion of the paper, to follow the student's progress. Thirteen reference staff volunteered to help conduct the survey.

During the middle part of the 2005 spring term, fifteen undergraduates were interviewed at the reference desks, and about a third of the students answered one or more of the e-mail follow-up queries. One student was interviewed in the science and engineering library, the remaining fourteen at the main humanities and social sciences library. Nearly all of the students were in classes that featured integrated library instruction; in one case, the professor was a member of the library staff. Most students were working under some time pressure, as indicated by reports of deadlines of one day to three weeks and by comments such as "the bibliography is due tomorrow," "paper is due," and "[need] to save time."

Some students were apparently feeling more than time pressure. One student explained, "It's hard to do research and I like to get help." Another reported, "I felt lost and overwhelmed about getting started." Although many students could correctly name the databases they had searched, others had developed their own terminology, such as "regular database" (the

Vicki Burns is Head, Rush Rhees Reference at the River Campus Libraries, University of Rochester; e-mail: vburns@library.rochester.edu. Kenn Harper is Biology Librarian at the River Campus Libraries, University of Rochester; e-mail: kharper@library.rochester.edu

libraries' online catalog, Voyager), "searched online" (Google?), or "search engine" (Voyager). One or two students were regulars at the reference desk: "I always come to the desk." What students generally learned in the course of the reference interaction with the librarians was the existence of specialized databases or effective ways to use the indexing of the databases.

In addition, some interesting commonalities stood out. Every student had already made an attempt to find information before seeking assistance at the reference desk. Although 20 percent reported using only Google, over half had used one or more of the databases provided by the library. In addition, many had e-mailed the librarian for an appointment, already knew the reference staff they met at the desk, or had a prior familiarity with the reference desk. In sum, these findings suggest that the typical student in our survey sample was familiar with databases other than Google, was under a certain amount of time pressure, and was either familiar with the reference staff in general or had been encouraged by instructors, friends, or family to seek library assistance.

After the survey was completed we conducted a process review that included the planning subteam, those who had participated in the reference desk survey, and other interested staff. We especially looked for factors that influenced survey outcomes. One factor was that we missed some potential interviews because of busyness at the reference desk. We also discovered that, although the questions were clear, sometimes the answers were not. For example, we had recorded answers such as "It was easy" to the question "What made it easy or hard for you to come to the reference desk?" or "I looked online" to the question "What print or online resources, if any, have you already checked?" Some interviewers felt uncomfortable both providing the reference assistance and conducting the survey about it.

These discoveries led us to spend some extended time thinking about the design of the questions, survey procedures, and methodologies. Other data collected by the Undergraduate Research Project indicated that some students never considered asking for help from the reference staff. After some deliberation we decided that we would gain more useful information about students by surveying them outside of the libraries, to reach those who usually bypass the services of the reference desk.

"Outside the Library" Survey

Having decided to expand our investigations beyond the physical library, we conducted a survey one evening in two locations where undergraduates congregate: the food court at the student center, and the main student computer center on campus. In particular, we sought to target undergraduate students in these locations who were actively working on a research paper.

Aside from following a prescribed schedule of questions (Appendix 2.2), the methodology for this second survey was very different from the first. In the student center we used a student employee of the library to cruise the food court and invite students to participate in the survey. A librarian then screened these students to ensure that they met the desired profile, and a recent anthropology graduate conducted the actual interviews. In the computer center, our staff anthropologist undertook all three roles. Because nonlibrarians conducted the interviews themselves, we hoped that the students would be more candid in their responses.

The interviews lasted approximately twenty minutes, and as a "thank-you" we gave the participants their choice of cookies, pretzels, soft drinks, water, or juice. We interviewed a total of fifteen students in the two locations, capturing their responses in notes as opposed to transcribed recordings.

Eight men and seven women participated in the survey. We do not have the college year for all the students, but know we had at least two seniors, three freshmen, and one junior. Our library student worker encountered no problems in enlisting students to participate. In fact, he had to pace his recruitment efforts to prevent a long waiting time for the actual interview. The academic disciplines were represented as follows: African American history, 1; anthropology, 2; brain and cognitive science, 2; computer science, 1; English, 3; history, 2; mathematics, 1; physics, 2; and religion, 1

The questions asked in the interview addressed how the students felt about their assignment and the methods they employed to bring it to a successful conclusion. We raised the topic of the library and reference librarians late in the interview to keep the focus on the student work practices and attitudes. The student perspective was paramount for us.

Survey Responses

Question 1: Do you feel you have enough time to finish this paper/project?

The overwhelming majority (87 percent) of students responded that they had sufficient time in which to write their papers. The two seniors who were writing honors theses were the only ones concerned about completing everything in the time they had left. One senior reported, "I'm, busy. I have other things I need to do for school, also need to relax, work, and do volunteering." Another responded that "it was assigned at beginning of semester so if rushed it is my own fault." Other students echoed this sentiment: they had the assignment early, and it was up to them to manage their work effectively to complete the assignment on time.

Question 2: How much do you really care about this paper/project?

All except three students cared "a lot" about this paper. Getting a good grade was important to them. For some students, their concern for the paper was driven by their interest in the topic. One of the seniors reported, "It's a culmination of the work that I have done for the last two years." Another student liked her topic and was interested to see how it would turn out. One student reported, "Initially I didn't care about it much; I became more interested while working on it."

One of the students who did not care much about the paper was taking the course for personal enjoyment and, though he wanted a "decent grade," he had other priorities to which he was applying his energy and time. Another said the class was a "requirement for my major, at first the material was interesting but is boring now, and I don't really care anymore."

Question 2-B: How well do you think you are going to do on this assignment?

All the students expected to do well on the paper. Forty-seven percent specifically mentioned that they hoped to get an A grade on the paper. Others mentioned that it was important to write a successful paper because it was a large percentage of their final grade. An intriguing response came from the student quoted above who did not care about his paper: "I will probably get an A because writing a good paper and being interested are different; helps to be interested but not necessary. I am motivated enough to want to do well in the class. It is not much more effort to write a good paper than a mediocre one, so why not write a good one?"

Question 3: How is it going? Are you finding all your books and articles/data pretty easily?

Sixty percent of the students had found articles and books for their papers; 27 percent (four students) had not yet found enough appropriate material. Two students had not begun their research. Almost half the students (47 percent) received recommendations for books and articles from faculty; 73 percent also specifically mentioned searching the library catalog and databases. Two students searched Google—one of whom said she had not yet searched the "library website." Several students reported mining bibliographies for additional sources. Some students found it difficult to find the "right" material for their papers.

The students had greater confidence about finding materials than they did about organizing and writing their papers:

"Just the fact that you weren't given a topic, no questions to answer, makes it a little stressful at this time in the semester."

"Lack of clarity from professor about the topic makes it difficult to come up with my own paper topic."

"The biggest challenge is figuring out what to say; that is not clear in my mind yet, but I have general idea that I am moving toward. I find devoting time and reading as much as possible is most helpful in getting to ideas."

"Coherency is the biggest challenge in writing. I have too much to say and find it hard to organize it. I think faster than I write. I put a lot of ideas down and it gets too random."

"The fact that I hate writing and feel pressure because I want to do well. It makes me not want to work."

These students understand the difficulty of writing the coherent, focused papers their instructors expect and report greater concern about organizing and writing than they do about finding books and articles.

Question 4: Have you asked anyone to help you with this?

Half of the students had consulted their professor or teaching assistant or planned to do so. Several commented that the professor was the best person to go to for help. Some students expected that their professor would review their papers before they turned in the final version. The other half had not consulted anyone. One student said that she "would just never ask for help unless [she] was completely clueless."

Twenty-six percent of the students mentioned that they planned to go to the writing center for assistance with their papers. These students were seeking assistance for the part of the paper they were finding the most difficult: the organization and presentation of their ideas.

Question 4-e: Did you think of talking with a librarian?

Of the fourteen students who answered this question, 79 percent had not talked with a librarian. Interestingly, 85 percent had worked with librarians in the past. From these responses we can see that once students have a research paper assigned they do not head straight to the reference desk for help. In fact, several in our sample lacked a clear understanding of the ways a librarian can assist them. Some students identified librarians only with print and with locating materials in the library collection.

Students reported successful assistance from librarians in the past. Our notes record one student saying, "Yes, librarians give more information about topic and give me more directions. Librarians are good." But the student quoted above as saying she would ask for help only when she was "clueless," responded, "I haven't used librarians; I would talk to a librarian when I need to find books. I can't imagine anything else I would need them for. If I was bad with technology, I would ask how to use the computer."

Another student responded: "I see them as people to help me find materials on paper. I probably asked a librarian at some point but found it mostly myself or from professor or other specialist. I went to the professor because they are the specialist in the subject area; I don't see librarians as specialists. They just know about general information. They are knowledgeable about search engines."

Question 5—When was the last time you worked on the paper? When's the next time…?

These students belie the idea that papers are written the night before they are due. It is clear from their responses that they divide the larger assignment into smaller tasks. One responded, "I worked on it today and this weekend I will find a source and do some reading." Another: "I haven't started; I will start by making sure I have articles by the end of the day—four days ahead and may start writing it then." Several noted that they would return to the research paper once they had other work completed. The responses to this question provide further evidence that these students manage their assignments well. They appear to maintain fairly good control of their academic work.

Survey Conclusions

Our goal was to learn about students, so we did everything we could to focus on their work habits and not on our workplace or ourselves. We met the students on their turf during their working hours (late evening) and inquired mainly about their work habits.

The students report that they are in control of their research and writing assignments. They are confident that they will do well, even when they have concerns about the organization of the paper. Those interviewed report that they work systematically through the research and writing process and organize their work so that they will complete their paper in the assigned time period.

These students depend upon library books, journals, and databases for their academic re-

search. Although they may begin a project with an Internet search, they understand that this search is not sufficient for their assignments. Many students are confident that they can find books and articles on their own, but they often look for recommendations from their professors and teaching assistants, whom they consider to be subject experts.

Some students, especially those who meet a librarian in a class, consult with a reference librarian about their research. Other students do not understand the role of a reference/subject librarian and associate librarians only with hard-copy materials and stack locations.

Outcomes

The students tell us that faculty are the subject experts. But although a professor may refer a student to a specific article or book and sometimes to a database such as JSTOR, s/he may not provide good direction for getting the student into the literature of the discipline. We consider this a vital professional responsibility for reference librarians, who know about current databases and library materials available to the university community. One of our greatest challenges, then, is to increase the undergraduates' awareness of librarians' subject expertise.

The most direct way to the undergraduates is through the faculty. Traditionally subject librarians have met with faculty members and attended faculty meetings, conferences, and seminars, serving as the main conduit of information about the library's programs and collections. Now we are expanding our librarian liaison role. Several subject librarians have office hours outside of the library, in their respective academic departments, where they meet with faculty and graduate students. Others are auditing entire classes, which enables faculty and students to get to know the librarians while the librarians get an inside view of classes and academic expectations. Strengthening the connection between faculty and subject librarians is a critical path to the students.

Our collaboration with the College Writing Center is expanding as well. Reference librarians have provided class-specific library instruction in the first-year writing classes for many years. In 2006 some librarians began serving as writing tutors. At the request of the director of the writing center, additional subject librarians will become tutors. In exchange, librarians give library research training to the other tutors, to the first-year writing instructors, and to the undergraduate writing fellows. We find that writing tutoring has helped with our work at the reference desk, particularly when the research and writing tasks are not differentiated by a student.

Several years ago we developed course pages with direct links to e-reserves that presented selected library resources appropriate for class assignments and a photograph and contact information for the subject librarian.[1] Many students request appointments directly from these pages. A similar program will be part of the Blackboard course-management system the university is now adopting.

We emphasized the role of subject librarians in two entertaining ways this academic year. Students told us that their parents often edit their papers and advise them about assign-ments, so we decided to get to know parents through the libraries' sponsorship of the parent breakfast held during the class of 2010 orientation. With posters combining Beatles songs and the theme "every class has a librarian," we discussed library programs and campus life with many parents and students. In addition, each year the libraries' host a Halloween Scare Fair. In the most recent fair, a fortune-teller asked students about their majors and then gave them a "ticket for success," which highlighted "their" librarian, a wise saying, and some trinkets. Believe it or not, students stood in a long line to meet the fortune-teller.

The Undergraduate Research Project has provided unique insights into the ways students do research and write their papers. We used the findings reported above, and other data collected in the overall project, to inform our public services retreat last year, at which we generated several innovative project ideas. We are meeting the students in new venues and building broader coalitions with campus departments. Although the Undergraduate Research Project has formally ended, we continue to use the skills we learned to update our understanding and gather new information about our students so that we may provide them with the best possible reference services.

Note

1. http://www.library.rochester.edu/index.cfm?page=courses.

Appendix 2.1. Undergraduate Reference Survey Worksheet

Place of survey: RR - Carlson - e-mail - Chat - Other

Surveyor:_____Date/Time:___

Person Surveyed

Name: E-mail:

Major(s):_____Year in School:_

Course:_When is the paper (etc.) due?_____

Topic of the paper/project:_____

When did they get their Gift? _Follow-up Dates 1)____2)_____

Question 1: What print or online resources, if any, have you already checked?

Question 2: Did you ask anyone else for help before you came to the Reference Desk?

Question 3: What did you learn during our session that was new?

Question 4: Why did you come to talk to the Reference Desk at this particular time?

Question 5: What made it easy or hard for you to come to the Reference Desk?

Remember the gift for the student and to request permission to follow up in 3 days.
Follow-up Questions

Initial Follow-up—Send by e-mail on third day after original survey.

Follow-up 1: After our session what additional resources did you look at—who else to you speak to?

Follow-up 2: Has another information question related to your paper/lab come up since we spoke and how did you go about seeking answers?

Follow-up 3: After you have turned in your paper, may I e-mail you with some wrap-up questions?

Final Follow-up Questions—Send by e-mail after the paper/project is complete.

Final 1: Over all how did the paper go?

Final 2: How did the help that I give you help you with the paper?

Final 3: Do you think that your grade was/will be influenced by the help that I gave you?

Appendix 2.2. "Outside the Library" Interview Questions

1. Do you feel like you have enough time to finish this paper/project? [Are you feeling totally rushed? Do you have time to do this properly?]

2. How much do you really care about this paper/project?
    a. Why? What do you really want to get out of it? [prompt for grades, knowledge, other, if necessary]
    b. How well do you think you're going to do [What are you going for? Is this as important as other assignments, or do you just want to get an acceptable grade and spend more time on other things?]

3. How is it going? Are you finding all your books and articles/data pretty easily?
    a. If yes—how have you been finding them? [What have you found? How did you find it?]
    b. If no—what have you tried? What has the problem been?
    c. All: Is anything else about writing the paper hard? Is anything else slowing you down or giving you trouble?

4. Have you asked anyone to help you with this?
    a. If yes—who?
    b. If no—do you have a reason for not asking anyone to help you?
    c. All: Who do you wish you could get help from? What prevents you from asking?
    d. Rather than face-to-face, would you like it better if you could get help on your paper/project through IM? Phone? Other technology?
    e. All: Did you think of talking to a librarian? Why didn't you? Would anything make you want to get help from a librarian? Have you ever talked to a librarian? Can you tell me where it was?

5. When is the last time you worked on your paper? How much later do you think you'll be up tonight? Will you work on this paper tonight? When's the next time you think you'll work on this paper? Where do you think you'll be the next time you work on this paper?

three. Night Owl Librarians: Shifting the Reference Clock

Suzanne Bell and Alan Unsworth

As librarians on a college campus, we often feel isolated from the lives of undergraduate students. They are our most numerous and visible patrons, but they have lifestyles and concerns very unlike ours. There is growing evidence that they study in different ways than we do and approach research in a different fashion. By their own account, they stay up much later than we do, fit many more activities into a day, and stay in constant touch with each other via cell phones, instant messaging, and other electronic tools. By the time they are ready to do research and writing, the librarians have gone home. Google, of course, never sleeps.

This is a professional problem, as well as the source of some social awkwardness. When combined with fewer reference interviews, declining circulation statistics, but a rising gate count, it suggests that we are becoming obsolete. As a building and a meeting place, the library is more popular than ever; as a provider of reference services, however, it is largely ignored.

How should we deal with this? At the River Campus Libraries we concluded that it would help if we understood our undergraduate students better. Many of us extrapolate from our own college careers to get some idea of the pressures (and the freedoms) undergraduates experience today. But a more current perspective is needed here, for technology and changing social norms are transforming college life. Through the Undergraduate Research Project we studied the behavior of undergraduates in

several ways. After many months of coviewing and sifting the accumulated data, we arrived at a crucial point. We needed to turn our findings into a few specific courses of action, and do it quickly, or we would miss our chance for the spring 2006 semester.

Since earlier studies indicated that many students use the library late at night (Albanese 2005), which was confirmed by our mapping diaries (see Chapter 7), we decided to pilot offering services on a schedule somewhat closer to theirs, to try to reach some of those late-working students. Librarians volunteered to take blocks of reference desk time from 9 to 11 p.m. to see if our services were in more demand then. Actually matching the students' schedules would have kept us in the libraries until 3 a.m., and we were not quite equal to that challenge. We struck a compromise between our aspirations and reality by staying until eleven.

We dubbed the pilot "Night Owl Librarians" and timed it for the end of the spring 2006 semester. The name was a particularly appropriate double entendre since the main social sciences and humanities library is known for the owl motif that appears in carved statues on its tower and in various grillwork and bas reliefs inside. It was a plan that was simple, inexpensive, and could be implemented in a hurry.

Planning: When, Where, How Late
Planning took only a couple of meetings and a small flurry of e-mail. The pilot Night Owl project

Suzanne Bell is Economics Subject Librarian at the River Campus Libraries, University of Rochester; e-mail: sbell@library.rochester.edu. Alan Unsworth is History Subject Librarian at the River Campus Libraries, University of Rochester; e-mail: aunsworth@library.rochester.edu.

would consist of librarians staying until eleven on Sunday through Wednesday nights. Experience and data indicated that gate counts in the library were too low to warrant staying late Thursday through Saturday nights. Both the main and science and engineering libraries participated. In addition to our physical presence, all of our publicity included the reference desk phone number and an IM screen name (askURlibrary), in case students preferred those methods of communication.

We determined to run the pilot for two weeks—the last week of March and the first week of April—the tenth and eleventh weeks, respectively, of our fifteen-week semester. Students arrived back from spring break the week before our first set of late nights. We knew that several classes would have paper deadlines approaching in that period and hoped that our intensive flyer campaign would make an impression in the week prior to Night Owl Librarian launch.

Figure 3.2. Night Owl advertisement

Whoooo's working late?

**Night Owl Librarians —
until 11 PM**

**Help with
assignments and papers**

Sunday – Wednesday
March 26 - 29 and April 2 - 5

Call:	275-4478 (Rush Rhees Reference)
	275-4465 (Carlson Library Reference)
IM:	**askURlibrary**

Figure 3.1. Night Owl table tent

Need Help?
Call: 275-4478
IM: askURlibrary
Night Owl Librarians
Sunday—Wednesday
until 11 PM

Publicity

It is a standard marketing concept that it takes at least five impressions to fix a product or name in consumers' consciousness. The one drawback to our schedule was that there probably was not sufficient time to advertise the new service to students. We did our best with the time available, and the materials devised by our reference department assistant, Diana Luce, certainly scored high on the "cute yet classy" scale (Figs. 3.1, 3.2). Using the basic owl design elements, she created flyers, signs to post

in the book stacks, table tents, and name badges. Hundreds of copies of the flyers were distributed to the residence assistants in all the dormitories and posted in the student center. Seemingly every level surface in both libraries got a table tent, and signs were posted throughout the book stack areas in both buildings. The flyer also worked perfectly as camera-ready copy for an ad in the student newspaper; one of the few identifiable expenses for the whole project was the $60 we paid for a 1/8-page ad. We also asked the editor of the student paper if the paper would be interested in running a feature story about the new service, a broad hint that was graciously received and promptly followed up on. The write-up was excellent: accurate and helpful. Unfortunately, both the ad and the story appeared in the March 30 issue of the paper, in between the two Night Owl sessions. It was not optimal, but at least it had immediacy.

Outcomes of the Pilot and Subsequent Sessions

After all our preparation and efforts at publicity, the experience of working during the later shifts

Table 3.1. Night Owl Service: Questions per Hour					
Session	Date	Sundays 4 hrs	Mondays 2 hrs	Tuesdays 2 hrs	Wednesdays 2 hrs
Initial Pilot	Week of March 26	2	2	1	.5
	Week of April 2	2.25	2	2.5	1
Unofficial add-on	Week of April 23	3.3	0	–	–
	Week of April 30	1.3	2	2	1.5
Fall '06 Re-run, Sunday/Monday only	Week of Nov. 19	2.75	1.5		
	Week of Nov. 26	Holiday	4		
	Week of Dec. 3	3.75	4		
	Week of Dec. 10	4	5		

turned out to be similar to our regular service hours. Students did not approach us because they had seen our signs, table tents, and so on or read the article in the student newspaper. They approached us because they happened to have a need, and we happened to be there, just as during regular reference hours. We did provide help to several people. The question that lingers for us (and that applies to all the subsequent times we have been Night Owls) is, Did we reach *different* people than we do during our regular hours? Because we did not quiz each student we worked with, we do not have an answer to that question.

The number of questions the desk fielded per hour is given in Table 3.1. It would not be appropriate to apply any sort of statistical analysis to these numbers, but we can at least say with some confidence that Sundays are a good night to be on duty into the later hours, whereas Wednesdays are not. Mondays and Tuesdays are mixed; they do not provide a discernable pattern. The amount of traffic we received during the two weeks of the pilot run of the Night Owls was enough, however, to make us respond positively to students' suggestions that we run the service again at the end of the term.

That period, dubbed "Unofficial add-on" in Table 3.1, was an almost completely ad hoc effort. It occurred in the fourteenth and fifteenth weeks of the semester and only on nights we were able to recruit volunteers—thus the irregularity in the nights and data. We did not do any publicity, not even table tents in the library. What does make these data interesting is that we have usage statistics for our regular working hours (9 A.M. to 9 P.M.) for the same days (Table 3.2). With them, we see an interesting jump in activity during the extended reference hours on Sunday, April 23: questions per hour during the day had averaged only 1.4, but from 7 to 11 P.M. we were helping an average of 3.3 people per hour. The same was not true for the next Sunday, however, and during the final days leading up to the end of classes the number of people seeking us out during the day was consistently higher than during our late night hours.

The fall 2006 Night Owls appeared with much less fanfare but far greater success, if we measure success by level of activity. The publicity consisted of flyers posted around campus, along with table tents throughout the main library, and having our icon (the owl) and announcement appear in the news section of the library homepage. In this round, librarians staffed the reference desk until eleven only on Sunday and Monday nights, for the

Table 3.2. Day Shift: Questions Per Hour				
Sunday 4/23/06	Sunday 4/30/06	Monday 5/1/06	Tuesday 5/2/06	Wednesday 5/3/06
1.4	1.6	4.16	3	3.8

last four weeks of the semester (weeks 12–15). We started the weekend before Thanksgiving (November 19) and continued until December 11, with the exception of the Sunday of Thanksgiving weekend. As noted in the "Fall '06 Re-run" section of Table 3.1, the busiest nights were the last two nights, the last week of the semester.

In general, this most recent iteration of the project showed more activity than any of the previous sessions, with the one anomaly of the third Monday night. The last two nights, representing the beginning of the last week of the semester, were our busiest yet. With our latest experiences, we think we may have found the right days and timing in the semester: Sundays and Mondays of the last four weeks of the semester. In all, our results are definitely enough to make us keep offering the Night Owl service.

Conclusion

Hindsight is, of course, always 20-20. Perhaps if we had started our advertising blitz before spring break, more students would have deliberately sought us out rather than find us by serendipity. But can we be sure that students would remember us after a week in the sun? We should not flatter ourselves by believing that students are thinking about librarians much of the time, if at all, and certainly not over break. Funding for one more round of the ad might have been helpful as well. On the other hand, academia does not handle on-again/off-again services very well. Moreover, neither students nor faculty are big on forward planning; they simply need you when they need you. So timing is everything. As it turned out in our pilot project, we did not hit the prime paper-writing time, despite our best efforts. To make up for this, we repeated our late nights during the last week of the semester, earning a moderate success.

In trying to decide the timing for the service, the most scientific method we discussed involved combing through every syllabus we could get our hands on, making a spreadsheet of paper due dates, and using that to determine the best weeks to run the service. Unfortunately, we have yet to do that analysis, and the best alternative seemed to be simply to try to cover smaller portions of more weeks at the end of the semester.

We have certainly learned that we do not need to keep the reference desk open all four nights. As noted above, the Night Owls appeared again in the fall 2006 semester, but just on Sunday and Monday nights. This reduced schedule helped because fewer volunteers were required (so we have fewer bleary-eyed librarians in the days following), which allowed us to offer the late-night service for several weeks rather than just two.

Sadly, even with the provision of free coffee and cookies during the pilot project, students at the science and engineering library remained stubbornly independent. Our Science Night Owls had only one encounter during the whole program, and they decided it did not make sense for them to offer the service again.

Finally, we learned that, although students are in constant touch with each other, their parents, and friends via instant messaging, our generic library IM name was not an effective way to reach them—or rather, for them to reach us. It got almost no use. What surprised us more was that the reference desk phone numbers got almost no use either. We know that people frequently get lost and confused in our stacks, and we thought they might welcome the idea of using their ever-present cell phones to call for help. But that did not happen either. In a way it is a positive: they are willing to come all the way back to the desk for the benefit of human assistance. However often it occurs, reference remains a social, person-to-person activity.

four. Library Design and Ethnography

Susan Gibbons and Nancy Fried Foster

In the very early stages of the Undergraduate Research Project it became evident that we would learn a great deal about the interplay of environments and physical facilities in the research and writing processes of students. Specifically, we saw an opportunity to learn more about where students like to study and why, with whom, and when. Consequently, three members of the project team formed a facilities subteam, which included other librarians and library staff whenever time and their schedules allowed. Initially, the subteam met weekly to coview student interviews, jointly analyze photographs, maps, and other artifacts, and share insights about the ways student research and writing are supported or constrained by libraries and other campus facilities. Our findings ranged from the expected to the surprising.

Impact of Library Facilities

We knew that a student's typical day started and ended later than the library staff's, but we were surprised to learn that there was almost a full twelve-hour difference between the beginning of a librarian's workday and when students generally begin their academic work. The main library opens at 8 A.M. and closes at 3 A.M.; the reference desk is open from 9 A.M. to 9 P.M. on weekdays, closing earlier on weekends. The students, however, settle into their research, writing, studying, and homework at around 10 P.M. and work very late into the night. This "night owl" schedule results from a combination of constraints and choices. After attending classes, working one or more part-time jobs, and engaging in such extracurricular activities as the Debate Club and the Medieval Society, students have literally run out of daylight hours. Between the demands of their schedules and the tendency for young adults to stay up at night, students adopt flexible schedules that change on a daily basis, getting up early one day, getting up late the next, sleeping on weekends, and working until one or two in the morning most nights. How can a library fully support the learning and research needs of students if it closes its reference desk precisely when students finally approach it? This is a dilemma that all academic libraries must face in the coming years.

We also learned about the different "zones" in our libraries. In some rooms, such as our Messenger Periodical Reading Room, you can hear the proverbial pin drop, even when full to capacity with 144 students. The reference area, in contrast, has a constant buzz and murmur. Level 500m in the stacks is quiet, but Level 300 is quite the party floor. Level A, to the left of the elevators, is for quiet, individual study, but group study can always be found nearby, to the right of the elevators. These zones are neither determined nor enforced by the library staff. Rather, the students develop and enforce them. Oldtim-

Susan Gibbons is Associate Dean of Public Services and Collection Development at the River Campus Libraries, University of Rochester; e-mail: sgibbons@library.rochester.edu. Nancy Fried Foster is Lead Anthropologist at the River Campus Libraries, University of Rochester; e-mail: nfoster@library.rochester.edu.

ers teach newcomers the established protocols through an occasional verbal warning, but most students tell us that they learned the rules as freshmen when upperclassmen gave them "the stare," a scowl or glare that communicates "be quiet!" Scores of signs reminding students to be quiet are not nearly as effective as one disapproving stare from a fellow student.

Through a variety of information-gathering techniques, we confirmed many of our hunches about student use of library space. For example, we put flipcharts out in public areas of the libraries with the following questions written on top: "Why do you like to come here? What is missing?" The thirty-eight responses students scrawled on the flipchart paper reiterated the need for additional power outlets throughout the building and better lighting in certain areas. The atmosphere, people, and quiet study areas were the most common answers to why the students liked to come to the libraries.

On the basis of these early insights, we made some changes and tried out some new ideas. For example, the Night Owl service, described in Chapter 3, is an attempt to address the time differences between the students' activity and the libraries' reference service hours. In addition, we created a new webpage that indicates the location of good study spaces within the main library.[1] The spaces are arranged by the "zones" that we discovered in the building: "Quiet," "Collaborative," and "Comfy." The webpage also identifies the locations of electrical outlets. Student comments on the flipchart suggested the need for stand-up, quick-use computers, where students could easily check their e-mail or look up a call number in the catalog. Consequently, we added three stand-up workstations near the main entrance of the stack tower.

The greatest impact of the Undergraduate Research Project on library facilities came in the second year of the project, which coincided with the initiation of a $5 million renovation of the east wing of Rush Rhees Library, the main humanities and social sciences library. Generously funded by the Gleason Foundation, the renovation project had two core objectives: to convert approximately 23,000 square feet of backroom library staff space into a collaborative study space for students; and to build a grand staircase to link the university's main student computer center, located on the ground floor of Rush Rhees Library, with the new collaborative study space to be built on the first floor.

Design Workshops

Although we had known for several years that the campus lacked appropriate spaces for group study and project collaboration, we had not known how to construct and outfit such a place. Now that our undergraduate project was learning so much about students and their work practices, the facilities subteam saw an opportunity to assist in the design of the space by bringing student perspectives and a student voice into the process. When we brought this idea to the dean of the libraries, he not only granted our wish but also upped the ante, charging us with finding ways to ensure that the space would meet the real, rather than the perceived, needs of students. Consequently, unlike a typical renovation project, we did not provide the architects with a formal space program that defined how the space was to be used, the numbers and types of seating, and so on. Instead, we asked the architects to work with us in finding ways to let the students drive the design.

We shied away from forming an official student renovation committee for fear that the formality might cause students to be narrow and too constrained in their thinking. Instead we crafted a more creative way to bring students into the design process, by inviting them to attend charrette-style workshops. A charrette is a technique in which stakeholders help to draft solutions to a design problem. In our case, the students designed ideal library spaces. Specifically, they were given a large poster-board, markers, pencils, sticky notes, and other supplies and asked to respond to the following scenario:

> Imagine that the library has a big, new, empty space—about the size of Douglass Dining Center—and they ask YOU to design it. You can put up walls or not have walls. You can buy furniture, hire staff, have the amenities and comforts that you want. It will be part of the library and it will be your place to use the library.
>
> So you design the space and overnight it is built. It is exactly the way you wanted it to be and you love it and want to go there a lot. Show us what it looks like.

We e-mailed several of the students involved in the Undergraduate Research Project to ask for twenty minutes of their time in exchange for some food, beverages, and $5. A few students showed up as a result of the e-mail, but we were far more successful in soliciting volunteers by simply putting up signs that read "$5 and Free Food for 20 Minutes of Your Time, This Way ➜." By the end of the two-hour period, we had nineteen fascinating designs by an unexpectedly diverse cross section of our student body (Figs. 4.1a and 4.1b).

Many of the designs had "creative" elements, including massage tables, fountains, gardens, and game tables, which was evidence to us that the students felt comfortable enough with the exercise to have fun with it and be imaginative. Still, in spite of the individual quirks, several common elements quickly surfaced. Nearly three-quarters of the drawings included "comfy" areas with such elements as fireplaces, sofas, beanbags, and ottomans. Fourteen drawings had group study areas that incorporated whiteboards, conference tables, and partitions or other structures to provide some level of privacy or sound dampening. Students sought support for their computer-based work, varying from actual computer workstations to strong wireless signals and *lots* of power outlets for their laptops. We could also see many windows, food sources, and even traditional library materials such as books and magazines scattered throughout the designs.

When all of the designs were distilled into a composite, we came away with five top findings. The first was the need for *flexibility*. Students like spaces that meet a variety of needs, and they want to move easily among these spaces. Most important among these spaces are group study areas, spaces to relax, individual study spaces, a café, a computer area, and media viewing areas.

Second, students want spaces that provide *comfort* and have a family room kind of feel. The Rush Rhees Library has an abundance of formal, straight-back chairs and massive wooden tables but a paucity of places to curl up with a good book. For our students, comfort includes easy access to coffee and food, natural light, and an environment with soothing textures, sounds, and great warmth. Moreover, the ideal space should support sitting, slouching, putting one's feet up, and lying down.

The third finding is the importance of *technology and tools* and their intuitive integration into the space. This includes high-end technology such as media players, Smart Boards, and plasma screens as well as low-tech items including staplers, power outlets, and a three-hole punch.

A fourth element students put into the space is *staff support*. Though only a few students drew a reference or information desk in their designs, a staff presence is commonly associated with food services and to "check things out," ranging from books to study rooms to staplers.

Figure 4.1a. Student design of ideal library space

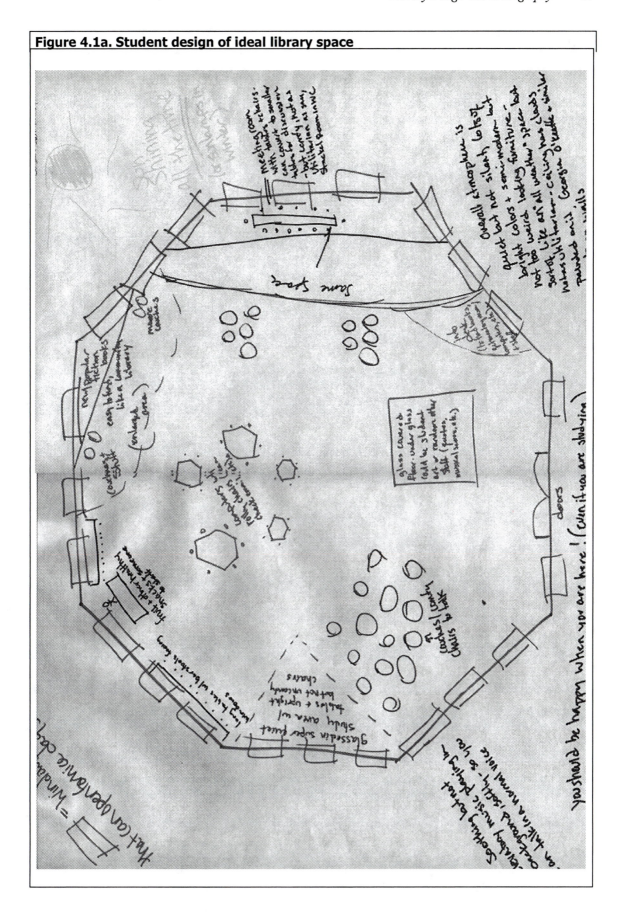

Figure 4.1b. Student design of ideal library space

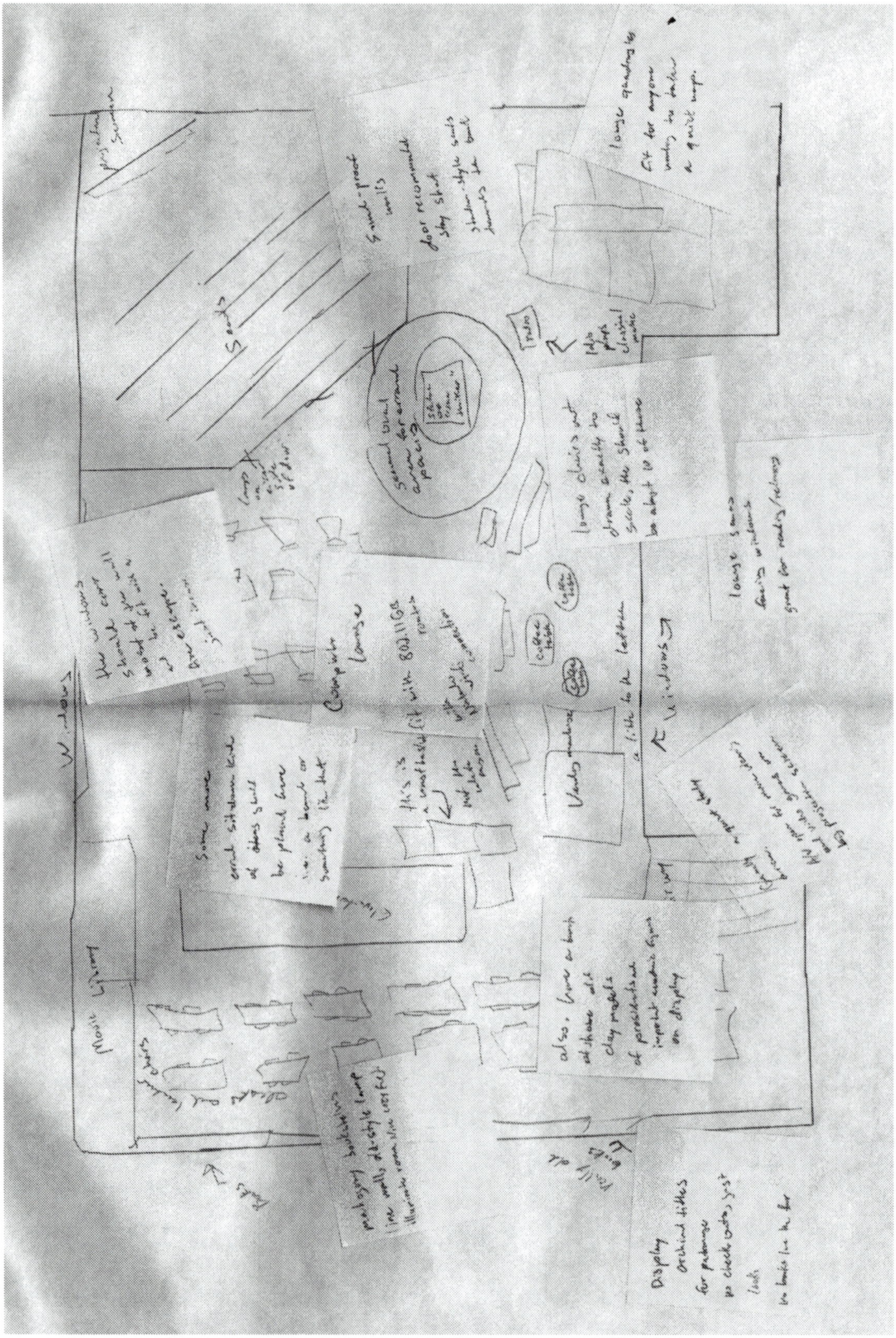

Students rarely make distinctions between the types of staff needed in the library. Instead, they include a generic staff person who is expected to provide reference assistance, check out materials, answer IT questions, and brew a great latte.

The fifth and final part of the composite is *resources,* and it is here that we are able to see some elements of a traditional academic library. Students included library materials in their designs, ranging from academic and reference books to leisure magazines and DVDs.

Armed with these findings, Susan Gibbons, a member of the facilities subteam, sat in on the interviews of potential architectural firms. The firm of Ayers/Saint/Gross of Baltimore was selected in part because it not only appreciated our desire for a student-centered process but, through a subcontract with furniture company Herman Miller, brought a new methodology to the process, called Future Pull. This is a way to poll customer representatives to identify the preeminent values driving the design of the space. Unfortunately, the Future Pull workshop could not be done with students because of timing. However, both Susan Gibbons and Nancy Fried Foster, the project's lead anthropologist, were able to represent student viewpoints in the exercise through the information gleaned from the initial student design charrette.

Led by Lori Gee of Herman Miller, the library's renovation team, architects from Ayers/Saint/Gross, and key university personnel envisaged a future several years after the completion of the renovation. We were asked to imagine that the library renovation was a great success and to articulate some of the elements that contributed to that success. After we developed a list of sixteen design elements—including comfort, intellectual stimulation, and great acoustics—we used personal response devices to rank each of the sixteen elements, as follows:

1. Integrated tools (seamless integration of high- and low-tech tools into the space)
2. Intellectually stimulating
3. Intuitive
4. Comfortable
5. Hub (a social and academic crossroads on campus)
6. Zones (clearly defined spaces within the larger space)
7. Rebootable (students can take temporary ownership of the space and personalize it, but when finished it can easily be "rebooted" to support the needs of the next group of students)
8. Great lighting
9. Experimental (space is meant to undergo frequent iterations as our understanding of the students' needs change)
10. Open outward (visually open space, with easy, visual access to the external environment)
11. Open inward (open and intimate, welcoming to individuals as well as groups)
12. Great acoustics
13. Memorable
14. Democratic (versus hierarchical. All are equally welcomed into the space)
14. Timeless
16. Unique

Furniture Design

Using the initial student findings and the results of the Future Pull workshop, the architects began designing our space. We quickly came to realize that what we were creating was just a shell, an open space of some 23,000 square feet. It was the flexibility of the space, the sound level, the lighting, and the furniture that we were going to put into the space that would make this a successful project.

Once we determined the placement of the staircase and the flow of traffic through the space, the architects asked the libraries' renovation team to do a simple "paper doll" exercise. The floor plan of the space was reproduced on large posterboards, and paper cutouts of different seating types, produced to scale, were provided. In groups of two or three people, we laid out the furniture in the space. Across the four designs, there was a great deal of similarity. However, cognizant that we needed student input, we asked the architects to hold off on any further furniture planning until we could gather student input.

We quickly geared up for a second design charrette with students. This time, we had two of our student workers recruit students randomly near the coffee cart in the Rush Rhees Library and in the student union. We invited students into the actual space and encouraged them to walk around and familiarize themselves with it. Then we gave them a plan of the space and a wide selection of furniture cutouts made to scale, along with markers, sticky notes, scissors, and glue. We told students that we

Figure 4.2a. Example of a student's furniture layout

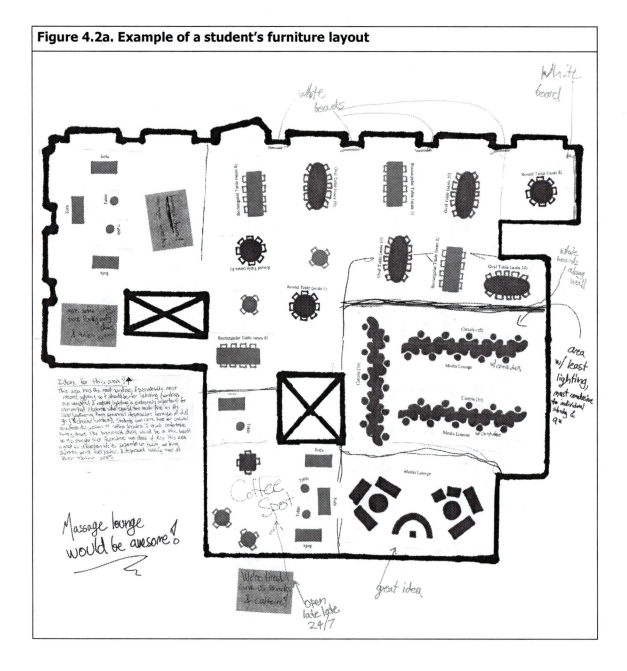

wanted them to help us design and furnish the space to meet their needs. We created some excitement by pointing out that they would be able to use this space—and see the fruits of their contributions—the following academic year. Once again, we provided snacks and paid $5 to each participant. In return, students gave serious thought and effort to the task of pasting the furniture cutouts onto the floor plans and annotating and enhancing the plans with additional ideas. These artifacts enabled us to learn more about the students' expected work practices in the space.

As we looked at the twenty-one resulting drawings, we found a vast amount of similarity (Fig. 4.2a, 4.2b, and 4.2c). What was striking, though, was how different the students' furniture layouts were to those done by the libraries' renovation team. If the furniture had been laid out as the renovation team proposed, we would

Figure 4.2b. Example of a student's furniture layout

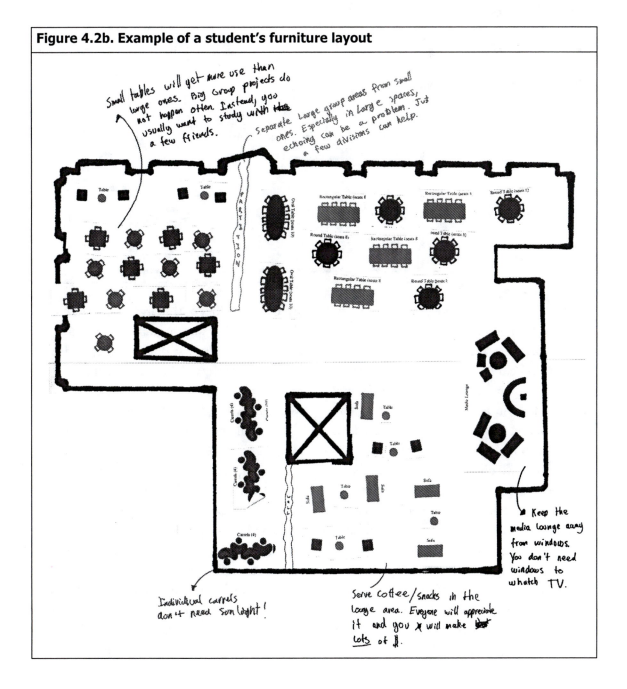

Figure 4.2c. Example of a student's furniture layout

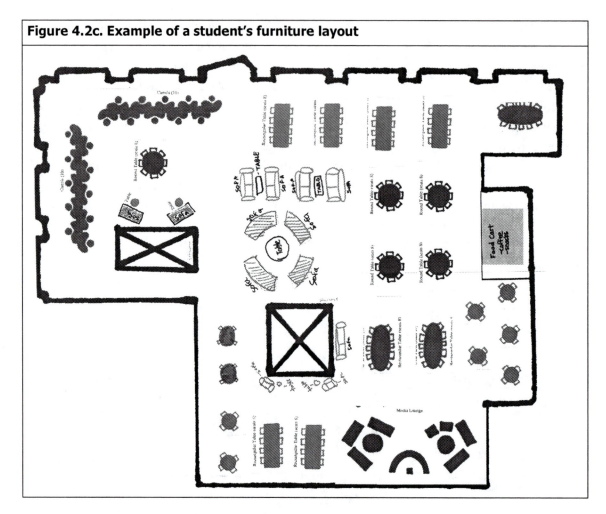

have simply gotten it all wrong! For example, four large, floor-to-ceiling windows will be added to the space, which currently has very little natural lighting. The renovation team had placed comfy armchairs and couches in front of those windows, imagining students curling up in the sunlight, reading their texts. The students, however, uniformly placed eight-seater tables in front of those windows. When we asked them about this placement, we learned that those large tables were desirable study locations because they provided plenty of space to spread out with one's laptop, textbooks, notebooks, beverages, and so on and be joined by one or two friends who are doing the same. Because students imagined that they would spend most of their time writing, researching, and studying at these tables, they wanted them in the prime

location—in front of the large windows. We also learned that students did not view these eight-seater tables as seating for eight students. Rather, they expected that no more than four or five students would be at any table, and this would allow for plenty of working space.

We would have made a second mistake had we gone with the renovation team's design by excluding quiet, individual study areas from the space. The Rush Rhees Library has literally hundreds of seats designed for quiet, individual study, and we assumed that they were more than enough; consequently we had focused on supporting group study in the renovated space. However, the student designs made it clear that in addition to group study spaces they felt the library needed additional quiet study areas. These were represented in the student designs with comfy seating and wall partitions. Just to ensure that we got the message, the students added notions to the designs including "<u>really</u> quiet study room," "area w/least lighting, most conducive to individual study & quietest area," and "comfortable, quiet area." Using everything this exercise taught us about student work practices and space use, we created a composite to share with the architects, and it became the starting point for floor plan.

Conclusion

The design charrettes taught us two important lessons. One is that gathering student input need not be a burdensome, time-consuming process. Each design workshop lasted for two hours and required approximately two hours of prep work and another four hours for analysis. The cost for each, beyond staff time, was around $100 in student payments and approximately $50 in supplies and snacks. Recruiting participants took little more than a few signs and an hour of student worker time. Going forward, we have learned that the logistics of gathering student input is far easier than we imagined and should never be an impediment.

The second lesson reinforced what we have learned throughout the Undergraduate Research Project, which is that we, as librarians, cannot assume we know how our students do their academic work or what they need. Over and over again, our assumptions have been proven wrong; these design workshops provide just another example. Had we based the design of the space on our assumptions about students, we would now be building a $5 million space which, though aesthetically pleasing, would not be nearly so useful to students as the one they have helped us design. Instead, our students—and our generous donors—can look forward to the realization of plans crafted through a creative and collaborative process.

Note

1. http://www.library.rochester.edu/index.cfm?PAGE=3469.

five. Dream Catcher: Capturing Student-Inspired Ideas for the Libraries' Web site

Jane McCleneghan Smith and Katie Clark

From the start, the Undergraduate Research Project has had three distinct lines of inquiry: the interplay of the libraries' services; facilities; and digital presence with the academic work of students. The focus on the libraries' digital presence built on our earlier study of how faculty find, use, and produce gray literature (Foster and Gibbons 2005). Just as the data gleaned from the faculty work-practice study had informed design enhancements of our institutional repository, we hoped that the findings from the current undergraduate project would inspire innovative uses of the libraries' virtual spaces and services.

In this chapter we focus specifically on two participatory design workshops conducted by the project's digital initiatives subteam. In the first one, students were asked to build a library Web site from the ground up. In the second workshop, students redesigned our current library Web site to fit their ideal. As we envisioned it, our libraries' Web site, like the one of Lakota legend, would be a dream catcher for our students' best ideas and, combined with our own, would help our undergraduates reach their academic goals and scholarly potential.

Participatory Design: The Workshops

A traditional Web design approach involves limited and late user input, which is typically solicited after a prototype has been built. In contrast, the River Campus Libraries employ a participatory design process, which brings the users into the design process much earlier—in fact from the very beginning.[1] The first phase of our participatory design process is discovery research. This step helps us go beyond our preconceived ideas of what users should need or might need to discover how users really work, what works for them currently, what they lack, and where they are frustrated. Once we have developed a concept of what we could build that would really benefit users, we go through cycles of engineering, usability testing, and refinement before putting the innovation, such as a new Web service, into use. The Undergraduate Research Project provided us with an opportunity to obtain more user data upon which to base future redesigns of the libraries' Web site.

We knew that undergraduate students used the Web, and we knew they used it in their academic work. What we lacked, however, was general knowledge of how the library fit into their use of the Web, and, specifically, how students used the library Web site. Moreover, we needed to know how Web services could help students do their academic work. Consequently, we designed the workshops to collect information about students' Web usage preferences without restricting them to currently available library options. The workshops allowed students to design their ideal library homepage while permitting us a glimpse into the students' online world.

Jane McCleneghan Smith is Library Assistant, Monograph Acquisitions at the River Campus Libraries, University of Rochester; e-mail: jsmith@library.rochester.edu. Katie Clark is Director, Science and Engineering Libraries at the River Campus Libraries, University of Rochester; e-mail: kclark@library.rochester.edu.

Table 5.1 Timetable for First Design Workshop		
Time	Type	Content
8:00–8:30	Individuals > small groups	Students fill out brief questionnaire when they arrive and then break into groups of three as they finish Create an electronic device Pizza and snacks as desired
8:30–9:00	Full group	Introductions ("coolest place you've been") Debrief
9:00–9:15	Full group	Brainstorming what to put on Web site
9:15–9:45	Small groups	Working on Web sites
9:45–10:00	Full group	Share
10:00–10:15	Full group	Conclude and pay
10:15–10:30		Wiggle room

We conducted two Web design workshops, one in the fall of 2005 and another in the spring of 2006. With each, the first order of business was to select the students to be invited. Drawing on a pool of participants from previous Undergraduate Research Project activities, we invited students by e-mail to attend one of the workshops. Sessions were planned for weekday evenings because few classes are scheduled then and our late-night visits to the residence halls and mapping diaries (see Chapter 7) showed us that students' energy levels would be high at a late-evening workshop. On the day of the second workshop, we recruited additional students by putting a sign on the reference desk offering free pizza and $15.00 in exchange for two hours of their time (see Table 5.1 for workshop timetable).

We reserved venues for the workshops in advance and chose them with the activities of the sessions in mind. The first workshop was held in a library reading room with comfortable chairs and sofas and several long tables. The relaxed atmosphere of this room was perfect for a lively brainstorming session, and the tables were well suited to the drawing and construction activities. The second workshop was conducted in a smaller, more intimate library conference room. This setting was conducive to the online coviewing activities that preceded the principle redesign exercise.

Food is always a useful incentive for student participation. We purchased assorted edibles and beverages ahead of time and ordered pizza immediately before the events. Other than refreshments, the only other supplies needed were a camcorder and tripod, a laptop computer, a projector, posterboard, markers and pens, sticky notes, tape, and scissors.

Each workshop consisted of four activities: a questionnaire to help us understand the participants' view of themselves and their relationship with the library; a warm-up exercise; a brainstorming session; and the main exercise. The main exercise for the first workshop was to have the students design their ideal library homepage from scratch, without looking at our current homepage. In the second workshop, students first reviewed the libraries' existing homepage and then based an ideal homepage on the model we provided.

Workshop One
Warm-Up Exercise
We began each workshop with a warm-up exercise designed to get the students to think creatively and feel comfortable in the workshop

setting. In the first workshop we asked two groups of three students:

> If you could have only one portable electronic device that did everything you wanted it to do, and you could magically make it small and light even while including everything you wanted, what would it be like?

The first group built an "Everything Machine." The students taped pieces of posterboard together to form a large box with four "screens." The four sides of the gadget—labeled School Supplies, Entertainment, Personal Health, and Miscellaneous—contained physical, electronic, and digital objects. The Miscellaneous screen included a cell phone, PDA (with scheduler), and how-to and self-help books. The Entertainment screen included a music and DVD library and a cable TV connection. A coffee machine, mirror, clock, toothpaste and toothbrush, and fold out bed(!) were included in the Personal Health screen. And last but not least, the School Supplies screen included a dictionary, thesaurus, language translator, stapler, tape, pens, and pencils. This fantasy device would be small enough to throw into a backpack. The students explained that the Everything Machine would be great for school because there would be no need to carry things like a dictionary or highlighters. The only thing it lacked was food, but, as the students pointed out, with the cell phone a food order was just a call away.

The second group designed a device that folded out like a flip phone, with gold stars representing different sets of functionalities: phone, calculator, calendar, camera, alarm clock, PC, television, TIVO, music, MP3 player, movies, lighter to make fire, thermometer, USB port, and Swiss army knife. Again, the device

Table 5.2. First Workshop Brainstorming, by Category	
1. Connect to library resources including librarians	
	Online catalog (books, catalogues, articles, DVDs)
	Subject area search engines
	Find movies/DVDs
	Subject area librarian
	Virtual librarian
	Food delivery in library
	Online slide library
	Books sorted by class
	When you login a list of your classes pops up along with a list of useful books
	PDF copies of all books and articles so you never have to leave your dorm room
2. Connect to class material including professors	
	Links to professors' sites
	Audio of class lectures in single centralized location
	Paper help with professor controls
	Virtual office hours, online chat with professors
	Search by department
	Chat rooms for multiple subjects
	Study group message boards
	Links to tests

Table 5.2. First Workshop Brainstorming, by Category	
3. Class Supplies and Support	
	List of everyone in the class so you can set up study groups
	Upcoming assignments (calendar)
	Assignment sorter from online syllabi (what's due?)
	Recommendations
	Course history of student
	Course planner (e-mailed work)
	Facebook list of people who took class year before so you can talk to them about the first test
	Download option to PDA
	Folder to save PDFs of articles, etc.
	Highlight PDF articles
	Ability to make notes in PDF files
	Ability to search through PDF files for highlighted text, note, and keywords
	List of figures and photographs
	Paper help with professor controls
	Major builder
	List of university policies
	Books sorted by class
	Automatically print out reserve articles when the assignment is due
	Connection to someone who will answer your questions about writing or grammar
	Calculator
	Translator
	Help Web (literary terms) for subject matter
	Dictionary
	Instant bibliography
	Dictionary.com
	Writing guides, e.g., MLA, APA
	Specialized dictionaries, e.g., biology, art history
	Grammar link
	AIM with grammar help
4. Connect to people and entertainment	
	Facebook, AIM
	Connect to your music, your personal library
	Radio station
	TV and movie schedules
	Movies and DVDs
	Newspapers, e.g., New York Times
	Order drinks online
	Food delivery in the library
	Bored.com
	Meal plan status
	Horoscopes

they designed was only slightly larger than a cell phone and would be easy to carry anywhere.

The warm-up exercise yielded useful information. The students' ideal electronic devices designed to do "everything you want it to do" did just that. Both devices had more than just entertainment and social tools; they also included academic and work resources. Both groups designed devices with library and academic resources as well as access to entertainment media and the functionality to stay in touch with friends (cell phone, camera). They even made sure that the essentials, caffeine and food, were part of their ideal electronic devices.

Brainstorming

After the warm-up exercise, we asked the students to do some brainstorming. In this group activity, students came up with suggestions for anything they wanted to see on the library Web homepage. They wrote their ideas on sticky notes, which we later organized into four categories: library resources, class materials, class supplies and support, and social and entertainment resources (see Table 5.2). Several items mentioned by the students are traditionally found on a library Web site, such as links to the online catalog and the capability to find books and articles. Many items, however, represented functionality and services that are absent from most library homepages. For example, they wanted to customize the library page so there were links not just to music but to *their* music. Another important element was food. The students were quite adamant that food (and caffeine in particular) should be available all the hours the library is open: "I need coffee, and deliver it to me in the library."

Another preference put forward was a single login to a list of their classes that they could sort by upcoming assignments. This included links to professors' Web sites and to online chat with their professors. They were also enthused about a tool that could create bibliographies, thereby saving them time, since it was "hard and tedious" to pull one together manually.

Table 5.3. First Workshop, Group One, Transcription of Webpage Design Drawing		
ACADEMIC Lecture recordings Lecture notes Course history of students Links to professor sites Chat with professors Folders to store viewed PDF's Links to old tests with answers		RESOURCE ACADEMIC Translator Grammar link Books sorted by class Catalogues for music books, articles, etc. Links to newspaper Search engines
		Instant bibliography Dictionary Study group message board Calculator TI-89
	UPDATES This section would include upcoming assignment due dates and similar alerts.	
NONACADEMIC Music Games Other Web sites Weather	(OPTIONS) Download option Print option Personalization options	ADMINISTRATION Major builder Course listings School policies (Study abroad, Take 5) Meal plan status

Table 5.4. First Workshop, Group Two, Transcription of Webpage Design Drawing

You are looking for...	Other links	Welcome (NAME)
Databases	My Folder	Image of Rush Rhees Library from Quad
Books	www.facebook.com	(Click "Enter" at the door and image will change to interior of library in 3-D)
Articles	Class resources	
Webmail	Librarians	
Resources	University hours	
My schedule		
My access		
Web CT		
Course catalogue		
Professors		
Chat		
Music		
Google		
Customize		

social resources. In fact, only a small subset of the links then on the libraries' actual homepage—to the online catalog, articles databases, newspapers, prior semesters' tests, and course reserve materials—could be found in the students' designs. Noticeably absent were links to e-journals and subject guides (see Tables 5.3 and 5.4).

We came away from this first design workshop knowing that undergraduates do use some, but not all, of our library resources. These students wanted to have access to everything they use (for work and play) from a single page and not have to travel to different university Web sites to accomplish different tasks.

Main Exercise

At this point, one hour into the workshop, we were ready for the main exercise. After the list of brainstorming ideas had been gathered, we asked the students to design their ideal library webpage starting from scratch. We gave the students the following assignment:

Using the ideas we just discussed and any more ideas you have, design a new library Web site. Include everything you would want to help you do your schoolwork and everything that would make your life as a student better.

The two groups of students organized their large collection of sticky note links from the brainstorming session into categories on their new Web site. In designing their ideal library homepage from scratch, students did not design one that linked only to library resources. Rather, the students pulled in links to other university academic resources as well as to

Workshop Two

Warm-Up Exercise

The main purpose of the second design workshop was to ask seven students to redesign the libraries' current homepage. Here again we started with a warm-up exercise. This time we asked students to design their ideal Facebook page after coviewing and commenting on a live Facebook page.

The students shared the desire to be able to customize the Facebook site by arranging their friends, much as they do with their IM friends list, and create their own categories of friends: cool people, nerds, friends who always have food, stalkers, high school friends, friends with a car, and so on. But they wanted these categories to be private; they did not want anyone to see how they had arranged their friends.

Brainstorming

For the brainstorming segment of the second workshop, we asked the students to look at posterboard mock-ups of our current homepage and do three things: cross off things they did not want, circle features they wanted to keep, and use sticky notes to add new things (Fig. 5.1). Using that as a basis, the students amended the libraries' homepage so that it represented their ideal site.

We were pleasantly surprised at the number of different links and services students wanted to keep on the homepage, such as Course re-

Figure 5.1. Students' critique of libraries' homepage

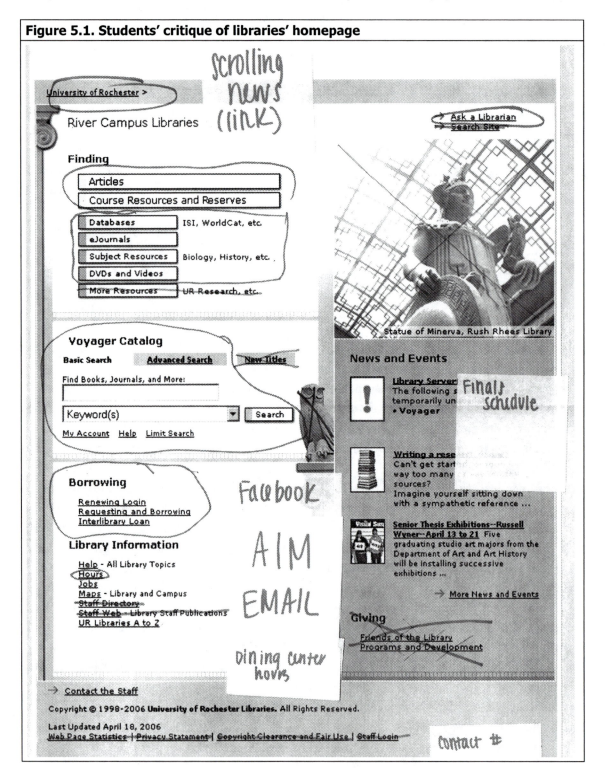

sources (for reserve reading and prior exams); Databases; Find Articles (a federated search box); Look for books; Renew books; Recall books; Reserve a room; and Interlibrary loan.

It was equally useful to see the homepage elements the students had crossed off. As with many academic libraries, we had a static picture on our homepage. The students immediately drew a big line through the picture; they hated it. Many wanted images that changed frequently, like the rotation of pictures on our university's homepage. Others thought the picture should be functional or removable if they did not want it. They also drew a line through the New Titles link because it retrieved too many titles to look through. And they crossed out the More Resources link because they did not know what it meant.

These undergraduates had plenty of ideas for what to add to the homepage. They quickly moved from a library-only page to one that did everything they needed, including, but certainly not limited to, library activities. Among their additions were:

- Shopping cart to save sources (books and articles)
- Software to convert saved sources to a bibliography in their preferred format
- Toggle link to subject librarians' webpages that could be turned on or off depending on the subjects of the student's current semester classes
- Map of the book stacks, since many students see the stacks as intimidating and a deterrent to using the library
- Any links and favorites of one's personal choice

They also wanted to add several university-related links including the final exams schedule, links to professors' sites, directory of professors' office hours and contact information, and an audio library of lectures as a means to take notes from missed classes. The students added links to social and entertainment activities, including live webcams, Facebook, AOL Instant Messenger, e-mail, scrolling news, and countdowns to Christmas, exams, and study breaks.

The students asked, "Where is the phone number of the library?" This was a huge surprise to us. We had made a deliberate decision not to include one on the homepage because we thought students primarily used e-mail and instant messaging to communicate. Obviously they *do* use e-mail and instant messaging, but most are never without a cell phone. They are just as likely to make a phone call to get the answer they need as they are to send an e-mail or text message.

Main Exercise

As the main exercise of the night, we asked participants to draw a new River Campus Libraries' homepage on a blank piece of paper using the mock-ups. Once again, students kept many of the current features on the libraries' homepage, especially those relating to reserves, the online catalog, and circulation. They also added new links relating to their schoolwork and entertainment and social interests. Some of the links were to already existing sites and services (e.g., translator sites, Facebook, dining center hours), but other ideas were purely imaginary (e.g., PDF versions of every book and journal).

Even more than at the first design workshop, we heard from students about how important it was to be able to personalize and customize the site. They wanted to be able to change the background colors and move items around on the page. They wanted to include a link to a subject librarian when they were working on a big research project and remove it when they were not. The Web site they designed ended up being all about "me," a site easily tailored to their personal needs and visual preferences.

Findings

Though the workshops were held six months apart and included different students, there were many common themes. In the first workshop, we asked the students to design a library homepage from scratch, without first looking at our current library homepage. In the second workshop, students first reviewed the existing library homepage and then designed their ideal site. The pages they designed in the two separate workshops were remarkably similar. Here is a synopsis of the main ideas:

1. Students chose to keep many of the links to existing library services. It was clear from these choices and the workshop discussions that the students did use the library Web site.

2. All participants placed additional links onto the library homepage. Some of these were to professors' Web sites and contact information and others were to departments on campus, such as the registrar and dining services. Some were for entertainment and social purposes, including music, instant messaging, and a food delivery service.

3. It's all about me. We knew this issue was important to our professors from our previous faculty work-practice research (Foster and Gibbons 2005), so we should not have been surprised to discover that the same is true of our undergraduate students. It was especially evident in the second workshop that the ability to customize and personalize was a high priority for students. They wanted links to *their* professors, *their* courses, *their* grades, and *their* assignments, and *they* wanted to control everything. They sought to take links on and off depending on the semester or point within the semester. They wanted to add "whatever would make the Web site best for me." These students have already used customizable sites such as My Yahoo, and they carry their expectations for this functionality to the library Web site.

4. In both workshops, what the students essentially designed was a portal. They want everything they need to be pulled together into a single place; it made the library resources more useful for them if they were also able to include other important resources. What they clearly did not want were information silos. Moreover, they did not want a generic undergraduate student portal, but one that they could customize and personalize.

Future Plans and Applications

We found that students do use online library resources and services, but that the library is just one small part of their total suite of resources. Through these workshops, we came to recognize "how the Library Web site is structured around the library and not around the students' far-reaching needs. In these design workshops, the library often appeared as a tool, but within the context of many needs and many tools" (Briden et al. 2007).

Our Web design workshops yielded brainstorming lists, artifacts, discussions, and drawings from which we hope to distill specifically articulated student needs and desires. This information will inform our work over the next year to redesign the library Web site.

We clearly saw that the students desired a portal, a single Web site that included library and academic resources, entertainment, social networking links, connections to faculty and their lectures, tools to manage their assignments and class work, and access to food delivery services. Consequently, building a student portal has become a high priority for the River Campus Libraries, which in the fall of 2006 began a partnership with University Information Technology to design a student portal that will include many of the personalized links and customizable elements undergraduates want.

We realize that many of our plans will take a long time to come to fruition. Still, we wanted to implement some changes right away. Adding the library phone number to the homepage was quickly and easily done. The boring, static homepage photo is now a rotating gallery of library-centered images, many featuring students. Thus, with a couple of small steps, we were on our way to weaving student-inspired ideas into the libraries' Web presence.

Note

1. More information about the River Campus Libraries' participatory design process is available through David Lindahl and Brenda Reeb's LITA Regional Institute workshop, "User Centered Design: Design Process and Usability."

six. Photo Surveys: Eliciting More Than You Knew to Ask For

Judi Briden

How many words is a picture worth? In conducting our Undergraduate Research Project at the River Campus Libraries, we have found that words and pictures in combination yield much more information than either alone. During the project we used a variety of methods that combined capturing images and words: retrospective interviews, photo surveys, mapping diaries (see Chapter 7), and video-recorded dorm visits. This chapter focuses on our experience with photo surveys.

In previous research by the River Campus Libraries on faculty use of gray literature, one of the methods we used was work-practice study, which borrows from ethnographic methodology (Foster and Gibbons 2005). We met with faculty in their offices or labs—the places where they actually did their work. Interviewing and video-recording them in these contexts captured a varied texture of details from which we could learn about their environments. Faculty would point to books on their shelves, papers on their desks, and documents on their computer screens by way of illustration as they talked about their research. They showed us their computer desktops and performed some of their work processes for us. Because we were there, we were able to ask questions about what they were showing us as well as capture images for later review and analysis. Using work-practice study as a method contributed significantly to our understanding of what faculty did.

As a result of this experience, when we began the Undergraduate Research Project, team members knew they wanted to talk with and observe students in their dorms—places where they lived and worked. At the start of the project, however, we felt we did not know our students well enough to know how best to approach them about making dorm visits. Until we could figure that out, was there another way to "see" students' environments through their own eyes?

Photo Survey

Some members of the project team were familiar with cultural probes from the work of Gaver et al. (1999), in which individuals were asked to reflect on and photograph their environments. Nancy Fried Foster, the lead anthropologist for the project, introduced us to the research done by visual sociologists, in particular the work of Douglas Harper (1984, 2001, 2006), whose photo-elicitation interview method provided a useful model. As Harper (1984, 21) describes it, "This method provides a way in which the interview can move from the concrete (as represented by the literal objects in the image) to the socially abstract (what the objects in the photograph mean to the individual being interviewed)."

Our project team decided to develop a protocol around the use of a disposable camera. We asked students who participated to take a series of photographs and then interviewed

Judi Briden is Digital Librarian for Public Service at the River Campus Libraries, University of Rochester; e-mail: jbriden@library.rochester.edu

Figure 6.1. Camera with list of requested photo subjects attached

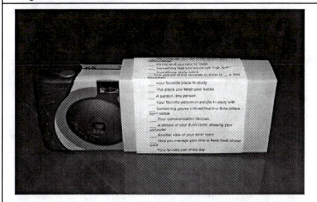

them about their pictures. We referred to this method as a "photo survey." We hoped that data gathered by this method would suggest new questions and areas for further research. We also thought that using cameras might appeal to students and engage them in a manner that was different from other investigations conducted for the project.

The process was simple. We created a list of things we wanted students to photograph, purchased a one-time-use camera for each student, attached the list to the cameras, and asked students to return the cameras when they were finished (Fig. 6.1). We had the film developed and transferred to CD and then scheduled an interview with each student to discuss his/her photographs. The interviews were audio-recorded and transcribed, so that the photographs and interviews could be reviewed and analyzed together by project team members.

In developing the list of photo requests, we were concerned to keep instructions to a minimum, allowing broad interpretation by each student as to what to photograph. This was a common thread throughout our research—asking open-ended questions that did not imply specific responses. In our planning, Foster characterized photo surveys as "a way to discover the unexpected, create artifacts that can be used as a basis for discussion, and learn about differ-

ent parts of students' lives we would not learn about through conversation."

So, what did we want them to photograph? The project subteams (reference outreach, facilities, and digital) brainstormed about what each would like to see from a student's perspective. Our ideas were prompted by questions we had after conducting a few retrospective interviews about research paper assignments, curiosity about students' dorm environments, and our interest in how they managed their academic responsibilities. The proposed photo requests were compiled and reduced to a single list of twenty:

1. The computer you use in the library, showing its surroundings
2. All the stuff you take to class
3. Something that you would call "high tech"
4. Something really weird
5. One picture of the libraries to show to a new freshman
6. Your favorite place to study
7. The place you keep your books
8. A person, any person
9. Your favorite person or people to study with
10. Something you've noticed that you think others don't notice
11. Your communication devices
12. A picture of your dorm room, showing your computer
13. Another view of your dorm room
14. How you manage your time or keep track of your work
15. Your favorite part of the day
16. The tools you use for writing assignments
17. The things you always carry with you
18. A place in the library where you feel lost
19. Something you can't live without
20. The night before a big assignment is due

The rest...whatever you want!

There were more than twenty exposures available in each camera; we wanted to reserve some for student serendipity. We also wanted students to consider this "assignment" fun, so some items on the list were meant to be intriguing—4, 8, 10, 15, and 19, for example.

Eight students participated by taking photographs in late 2004 and the first half of 2005. They were recruited individually— some by asking students who were already participating to refer their friends. They completed the assignment at different times, and we paid each student a small amount. As the student returned his/her camera, we scheduled a follow-up interview, allowing sufficient time to develop the images and transfer them to CD. In the interview, which was audio-recorded, Foster and the student viewed the images on a computer screen and talked about them. Viewing images on the computer made it easier to talk about what was depicted and was more comfortable than huddling over a snapshot. Often, after the student described what the photo represented and was prompted for amplification, Foster would then comment in an open way about something else in the picture or expand on what the student had said by asking about the same thing in other contexts. Often, it was this gentle, follow-up probing,

Figure 6.2. Student A's "favorite place to study"

Figure 6.3. Student B's "favorite place to study"

rather than the initial question, that elicited the greatest detail. As an example, the following is an excerpt from an interview about a picture showing "your favorite place to study":

Foster: And this is "your favorite place to study"…

Student A: This is our study lounge; there is where I study for all my exams. I only have exams in one class, but that's where I study for them.

Foster: And this is on the first floor of [your dorm]? Are you usually in there alone?

Student: No, when I'm studying for science I have my friend [name] and usually when we do work in here, we work together because it's better to have somebody in there with you because you can talk and take a break…

Foster: Are there times when there are many people in there studying many different things?

Student: Not really, because usually when somebody goes in there, if there's people

Figure 6.4. "A place in the library where a student feels lost"

in there, they won't stay in there, they'll leave.

Foster: So it's sort of like an unwritten rule that if there's some people in there studying together, it's sort of taken?

Student: Well yeah, because you don't want to be in there with people talking, you probably won't go in if there's other people. And also people have different times when they're working, and we like to work between 8 and 1, and usually other people go to the library or they'll work in the afternoon.

Foster: You're talking about 8 A.M.?

Student: No, 8 P.M.

Foster: At that hour, most people are doing something else?

Student: They're usually in the library. Most of our hall likes to work in [the main campus computing center in same building as the library]. Or they'll be in their room or dinner or watching something.

Foster: So, as it works out, you and your friend are pretty much the ones who want this space at that time. Have you ever had to go somewhere else?

Student: No, we've never had to go somewhere else.

From an interview with a different student:

Student B: …that was my favorite place to study. Or, not my favorite place to study, well I guess that's what the question is called. I wouldn't call it my favorite place to study but I took a picture of the upstairs level of [the main campus computing center in same building as the library] because I like the atmosphere there. It's more of a group study atmosphere, it's more casual, you're allowed to chat. I studied a few times in the Great Hall [in the library] in the quiet, respectful places, but I don't think I'm as constructive in those places. My mind ends up wandering.

Foster: When it's quiet your mind wanders, because you're distracted by the quiet?

Student: Yeah, or I end up with music of my own stuck in my head sometimes, or in any case, unless I'm really into what I'm reading I'm not going to be able to do it in a quiet setting. So for a lot of studying, especially if it's something I can study group-oriented, I do it here.

In these two excerpts, students are expressing very different needs. One wants a quiet place to study, and the other cannot study if it is too quiet. The entire project reinforced for us the importance of understanding and accommodating the diverse needs of our students.

One student's photograph and discussion about "a place in the library where you feel lost" made us wince:

Student:… I am still having a hard time negotiating the library. So, whenever I get there, I am trying to figure out where I am going. So I just stare at this list [guide to library stacks, posted by every elevator] and figure out where I have to go.… I feel very lost. Where am I going? Am I even at the right elevator?

Foster: You might *feel* lost when you are standing here—have you ever actually *gotten* lost?

Student: Yes, I got lost in the stacks, and I had to find somebody else, get them to help me get out because I didn't know where I was. It was very upsetting. I am usually pretty good with landmarks, so if I get myself somewhere I can usually get myself back. This time I had been meandering, and I pop out of the stacks and there was no one and no exit signs. This is the ultimate worst freshman moment.

Foster: So somebody just sort of appeared?

Student: No, I just wandered until I found someone. And I was like, "Hi, sorry to bother you. You look like you're studying pretty hard, but I don't know where I am. And I don't know how to get out, and I have an appointment in fifteen minutes." They were like, "You're a freshman?" And I was like, "Yeah."

Like most large university libraries, ours is a complex environment. Over the years, we have looked for ways to improve signage and other aids to wayfinding. We currently use a variety of tactics including maps, contextual signs, inclusion in bibliographic instruction, help desk assistance, tours, and special events that attract students into the stacks. This student's experience reminds us that we need to be doing more.

The photographs taken by students of their rooms, desks, bookshelves, and computers were the most productive for eliciting details during the interviews. As we asked questions about what we could see in the images, we learned how students did their work and what they did for recreation and relaxation. We learned about social interactions with roommates and floor mates and friends. The many objects shown, and their juxtaposition, prompted us

Figure 6.5. Two students' photos of "a picture of your dorm room, showing your computer"

to ask questions we had not anticipated, but that turned out to be very informative. As well, these images helped us appreciate our students as individuals with different personalities, preferences, and unique environments. Figure 6.5 shows two of the many images we studied.

After each interview had been completed, team members met to coview photos and listen to the audio recording. Exposure to the data as a group contributed to our shared understanding and discussion of what we were seeing, how it related to data from our other investigations, what additional questions were raised but not answered by the interview, and what points we thought were most important to take away from the session. Further analyses were undertaken by team members during the course of the project—to look at details of students' rooms and computers for common or unique elements, to compare what different students carried to class, and to review the varied ways students kept track of their work. Throughout the project, we encountered data from different investigations that supported specific findings. Having disparate data inform a single conclusion reaffirmed for us the value of using different methods.

Lessons Learned

Photo surveys as a method worked quite well in eliciting useful data. Combining the visual and the oral provided us with more opportunities to question and learn. We did, however, encounter a few problems. We think that most of these problems could be reduced or eliminated in the future.

A camera's flash did not always work for every photograph. As a consequence, some images were too dark to show much detail. When this happened, students were sometimes able to say what the photographs were supposed to be and to recall what they were thinking when they took them.

Another problem was the time delay between a student taking his/her photos and the interview. A student might have forgotten, or at least be vague about, why s/he took a particular shot. Overall, however, students were articulate about most of their photos. And since the images prompted questions, they were still useful for eliciting information.

A third problem we encountered was difficulty matching a student's photos with items on the list of photo requests. When we created the list, by numbering them we implied a specific sequence. At first, we actually asked students to take pictures in the same order as the list. In preparing the list, however, we failed to evaluate the convenience of this sequence for the students. When they were in their rooms, it might be easier to take 2, 7, 11–14, and 16–17 together. Items 1, 5, and 18 might be easier to photograph in a single visit to the library. Once we realized this, we replaced the numbers on the list with blank lines and asked students to fill in the number of each photograph as they took it. This was an improvement, but it was still difficult at times to match the list with the sequence of images on the CD. Further, when the project team reviewed the interviews later, we had to coordinate recorded interview segments, images, and list.

Findings

What did we learn from the photo surveys? Some findings provided answers to specific questions we were asking, some gave us hints that were confirmed through other investigations, and others were completely unexpected. We were surprised to discover how willing students were to show us and tell us about their lives. Their comfort reduced our anxiety about asking them to take part in the research. As a consequence, it was easier to pursue other questions and to develop different protocols. At the same time, we became more sensitive about protecting the confidentiality of

Figure 6.6. Student's photo of "how you manage your time or keep track of your work"

these students who were so open with us, even if they were unconcerned on their own behalf.

Having already conducted several retrospective interviews, we suspected that students were quite busy and used a variety of techniques to keep up with their academic and social commitments. Photos of "how you manage your time or keep track of your work" confirmed this (Fig. 6.6). One student took a photo of his head to show how he kept track, and another described the merits of Linux calendaring software to integrate personal and academic responsibilities. Most students used more than one tool to keep up with their lives. One recorded assignments three different ways—in a class notebook, with computer scheduling software, and on a PDA. Another used a planner and multiple sticky notes posted around her desk. One first-year student had already recorded in a notebook (her "life binder") all of the courses she would take as an undergraduate, organized by major and cluster, and which semesters she would be taking them.

Combined with the results of two other investigations, mapping diaries (see Chapter 7) and dorm visits, we came to understand that students were actually on the go day and night and were seldom focused exclusively on any one activity. Academic, social, recreational, work,

volunteer, and personal activities were all in the mix, and each day was different.

We were very interested in the technologies students had available and which ones they actually used. Photo request items 3, 11, 17, and 19 were intended to elicit this type of information. Computers and cell phones were most common. MP3 players showed up in some photos or were mentioned in the interviews. Only one student we interviewed for photo surveys used a PDA. On their computers, many students used e-mail, instant messaging, and Facebook or MySpace. During dorm visits later in the project, we followed up with more questions about what was on students' computer desktops and the activities associated with having them there.

In asking about communication devices, we discovered that "landline" telephones supplied by the university in dorm rooms were not used at all or were relegated to use only in limited circumstances (e.g., for calls within the dorm and to save on long distance charges from cell phones' out-of-state numbers). One student described occasionally finding messages on his room telephone long after they had been left, simply because he never thought to check it. Everyone he knew called him on his cell phone. Overall, multiple communications technologies were used by students, but the specific ones varied from student to student. This has implications for libraries trying to choose the best means to communicate with their students.

In one instance, it was the absence of something that caught our attention. In photographs showing "all the stuff you take to class," we observed that laptops were not included, even though students had laptops (see Fig. 6.7). So, we noted it down without understanding why, until the mapping diaries, with more data about students' days, provided an answer (see Chapter 7). That is when we discovered how itinerant students were during the day, carrying what

Figure 6.7. Two students' photos of "all the stuff you take to class"

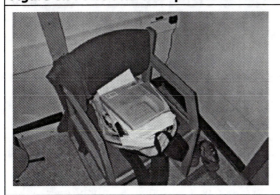 

they needed for long stretches. They covered a lot of territory, and it simply was not practical for most to include a laptop along with all the other things they brought to classes. Instead, laptops came out when students planned to be in one place for a while to do their work, such as in the library at night.

When we combined our data from visiting the dorms with the photo surveys, it became easier to understand why our library buildings were so popular with our students for working for long periods on assignments. Friends going in and out of rooms, impromptu activities down the hall, games, music, and phone calls—these were just some of the distractions working against getting assignments done. The library provided a refuge when students just *had* to work.

Through photo surveys, our students shared details about their lives in a way that conventional interviews alone could not achieve. They showed us their rooms and the places they liked to go, their friends and study buddies, their possessions and preferred work environments. For library staff, the images and interviews pulled together varied facets of being an undergraduate at the University of Rochester that were previously unknown to us and made them real and cohesive. We now understand much more about our students' lives beyond the doors of the library.

seven. Mapping Diaries, or Where Do They Go All Day?

Katie Clark

Why do students still use the computers in the library when we know they all have one in their dorm rooms? Why is there a steady stream of students coming in the library door at 9 P.M.? Simple mapping diaries turned out to be a rich source of information about these and other student behaviors with implications for academic libraries.

In our project to discover how undergraduate students worked (i.e., wrote papers) and lived, we used a variety of techniques to gather information including interviewing students about their paper research and writing techniques, visiting dorm rooms to see what they had on their computers, and giving students disposable cameras with which to take pictures of their environment (see Chapter 6). We also asked the students to keep a "mapping diary" and record where they went during a schoolday, which is the focus of this chapter. Fourteen students kept these diaries, and the results were surprising.

Background

One of the great challenges of studying students is getting access to them when they are actually doing their academic work. Their most productive hours tend to be outside the librarian's normal workday. Moreover, students do much of their academic work in their dorms, friends' rooms, lounges, student centers, and even empty classrooms. Further complicating our task, students approach their academic work and their social lives as one integrated collection of activities. To understand how students research and write their papers, we needed to understand how they fit their paper-writing activities into the overall flow of their lives, as they move from place to place and activity to activity, throughout the campus and throughout the day.

Anthropologist Michael Moffatt (1989), who conducted seminal research on college life at Rutgers University, asked students to draw maps of the university campus to help him understand their cultural construction of the landscape. For our project, we melded Moffat's approach with another anthropological technique, the time allocation study, which we knew through the work of Daniel Gross (1984). We gave students a map of the campus and key surrounding areas and asked them to mark their movements on this map, indicating when they arrived at each place and when they left it. The resulting maps gave us a record of how fourteen individual students spent an actual day of their lives.

Procedures

We recruited our first group of nine students in the fall of 2005 through other research activities in our project. For example, students who participated in our interviews or design workshops were randomly asked whether they would be willing to take a map and, for a $10 research subject reward, mark down their movements over the course of one day and then allow us to

Katie Clark is Director, Carlson Science and Engineering Library at the University of Rochester; e-mail: kclark@library.rochester.edu